The Hidden Tyranny Of Our Money

What Most Economists Don't Know
And Few Wish To Tell

Víctor Gómez-Enríquez

The Hidden Tyranny Of Our Money

What Most Economists Don't Know
And Few Wish To Tell

Víctor Gómez-Enríquez

ISBN-13: 978-1-910881-99-6

This edition printed by
Amazon CreateSpace
for exclusive sale and distribution by
Amazon.com, Inc. and its affiliates.

Black House Publishing Ltd
Kemp House
152 City Road
London
United Kingdom
EC1V 2NX

www.blackhousepublishing.com
Email: info@blackhousepublishing.com

To Jorge and Olivia

"By this means the government may secretly and unobserved, confiscate the wealth of the people, and not one man in a million will detect the theft." — John Maynard Keynes, *The Economic Consequences of the Peace.*

Chapter I

Introduction

This book is the result of the author asking some basic questions about the economic crisis in 2008. What was the origin of the financial crises such as those in 1929 and 2008? Are they really inevitable? — a natural feature of a "free-market" economy? Or are they avoidable ? and if so what can we do to prevent them?

The official explanation is that the economies in this world are subject to cycles of booms and busts that happen more or less regularly and are inevitable. However, nobody speaks about the role of the monetary system in all of this or, more specifically, whether the kind of money that we use has any effect in economics.

One exception to this rule is given by the Austrian School of Economics whose major exponent is Ludwig von Mises[1]. According to this school, economic cycles are the result of artificial credit expansion via what economists call fractional reserve banking. Simply explained, this means that in a first stage and in a context of low interest rates set by the central bank, commercial banks create excess money out of thin air, that they lend at interest, and this produces false signals in business opportunities that provoke so called malinvestments (badly allocated investments) on the part of entrepreneurs. Then, on a second stage, when the market exposes these bad decisions, a depression takes place that tries to correct what went wrong and restore equilibrium again.

The fact that most of the money, around 97 per cent of the

---

1   von Mises, 1996, Ch. 20

money supply, that we use today is created by fractional reserve banking supports the Austrian theory of the business cycle. Imagine that one creates a lot of dollar bills by using a printing press and one introduces this money into the economy little by little, starting with family, friends and people that one trusts most. What would be the effect of this action? Has the economic community more wealth because it now possesses an additional heap of money created out of thin air? Is it not natural to think that the people who have received some of this extra money will start increasing spending accordingly? For example, a group of real estate entrepreneurs might overestimate housing demand because there is an excess supply of money that has been artificially created, so that they therefore decide to build too many houses, thus creating a housing bubble. When the bubble pops, a depression takes place that tries to lead the housing market into equilibrium again.

Very few people know that all money in existence has been created out of debt and most of it by commercial banks through fractional reserve banking. Only a tiny portion is created by the central bank. We will describe the process in more detail later in the book. Suffice it to say in this chapter that, since the creation of money implies a debt, for each dollar that is created into existence, we must return an amount equal to this dollar plus the interest. Thus, when we pay our debts, we withdraw more money from circulation than was created.

Fractional reserve banking allows commercial banks to create money out of nothing by making loans. This leads us to the distinction between usury and interest, which will be addressed later in the book. For the moment, we will say that interest refers to the increase of wealth overtime due to fruitful human labour, whereas usury is the result of demanding some goods and services after a period of time from a loan of something that has no intrinsic value. For example, if I lend something valuable, called the principal, to someone and demand that after some time the principal be returned together with some goods and services, this additional last part is the interest. If, on the other hand, I create some money out of thin air and I lend it at interest, this is usury. Thus, usury in our view does not mean excessive interest in loans, which is the traditional definition in our times, but a way of earning some profit from a fraudulent loan.

One problem with the Austrian school explanation of the business cycle is that it is not the mainstream one in current economics. On the contrary, we can say that very few economists give credit to the Austrian school of Economics. This is the reason why almost no one speaks in the mainstream media about the Austrian theory of the business cycle.

Apart from the Austrian school, there have been some people in politics, academia and business who have seen something unscrupulous in our monetary system. For example, the famous British economist John Maynard Keynes, referring to the monetary system, wrote in *The Economic Consequences of the Peace* [2] that:

> "By this means the government may secretly and unobserved, confiscate the wealth of the people, and not one man in a million will detect the theft."

The British Nobel prize laureate in Chemistry (1921) Frederick Soddy also studied economics and stated in his book *Wealth, Virtual Wealth and Debt* [3] regarding the monetary system that:

> "If we reasoned similarly in physics, we should probably discover that weight possessed the property of levitation."

Henry Ford (1863-1947), founder of Ford Motor Company, is quoted as saying that:

---

2   Keynes, 1920

3   Soddy, 1933

Introduction

"It is well enough that people of the nation do not understand our banking and money system, for if they did, I believe there would be a revolution before tomorrow morning."

Thomas Edison (1847-1931) was ardently opposed to the gold standard and debt-based money. Famously, he was quoted in the *New York Times* stating "Gold is a relic of Julius Caesar, and interest is an invention of Satan."[4]

Sir Josiah Stamp, director of the Bank of England (1928-1940), while speaking at the University of Texas in 1927 is quoted as saying:

"The modern banking system manufactures money out of nothing. The process is perhaps the most astounding piece of sleight of hand that was ever invented. Banking was conceived in inequity and born in sin ...; Bankers own the earth. Take it away from them but leave them the power to create money, and, with a flick of a pen, they will create enough money to buy it back again ...; Take this great power away from them and all great fortunes like mine will disappear, for then this would be a better and happier world to live in ...; But, if you want to continue to be the slaves of bankers and pay the cost of your own slavery, then let bankers continue to create money and control credit."

Congressman Louis T. McFadden, Chairman of the House Banking and Currency Committee, in a speech on 10th June, 1932, said that:

"Some people think the Federal Reserve Banks are U.S. government institutions. They are not ...; They are private credit monopolies which prey upon the people of the U.S. for the benefit of themselves and their foreign customers, foreign and domestic speculators and swindlers, and rich and predatory money lenders."

---

4   "Ford Sees Wealth in Muscle Shoals", The *New York Times*, December 6, 1921

John Kenneth Galbraith, former professor of economics at Harvard, stated in his book Money: *Whence it came, where it went* [5] that:

> "The study of money, above all other fields in economics, is one in which complexity is used to disguise truth or to evade truth, not to reveal it. The process by which banks create money is so simple the mind is repelled. With something so important, a deeper mystery seems only decent."

Milton Friedman, Nobel Prize winning (1976) market economist, is quoted as saying in a National Public Radio interview (Jan 1996) that:

> "The Federal Reserve definitely caused the Great Depression by contracting the amount of currency in circulation by one-third from 1929 to 1933."

At the Conference to Honour Milton Friedman held at the University of Chicago on 8th November, 2002, the then Governor of the Federal Reserve Board, Ben S. Bernanke, stated:

> "Regarding the Great Depression. You're right, we did it. We're very sorry. But thanks to you, we won't do it again."

Finally, Martin Wolf, Chief Economics Editor of the *London Financial Times*, wrote on 9th November, 2010 that

> "The essence of the contemporary monetary system is the creation of money out of nothing, by private banks' often foolish lending."

In view of the previous quotes and remarks, we can say that some very intelligent and well informed people have considered our present monetary system as deceitful, inefficient, and presented to the public in a way that makes it appear very complex when

---

5   Galbraith, 2001, Ch. 1

in reality it is not. It seems that it has been conceived as an instrument to cheat on the public so that they are robbed by a clique of bankers and politicians without being aware of it.

In this book we will show that this is indeed the case. That our monetary system is flawed and it is the main cause of the recessions of 1929 and 2008 and the rampant inequalities in society today. But not only that. The present monetary system confers immense power to an elite that controls the money supply and uses this power in turn to buy all important communications media, install presidents in governments, dictate the main trends in academia, and decide the course of geopolitics in the world.

This is the reason why nobody speaks nowadays about the influence of the monetary system in economics, politics, etc. Because if someone does, he or she would instantly commit "career suicide". In other words, if a prestigious university professor or a famous journalist would dare speak about the evils of our present monetary system, he or she, would be immediately discredited and probably fired. In this context, it is to be noticed that criticism of our monetary system has been decreasing since 1913, the year in which the Federal Reserve Act was passed, and especially since 1971, the year in which the Bretton Woods system was brought to an end by President Nixon's defaulting on his obligations (Nixon shock), so that it is very hard to read or hear something critical of the system today. This indicates that the control of mainstream media by the elite is much more powerful today than it was in the past.

In the rest of the book, we will first address in Chapter 2 the question of money. How it is defined and what kinds of money have been used throughout history. We will also make the distinction between sound and unsound fiat money.

In Chapter 3, we will examine some examples of successful fiat money in history to show that the use of fiat money does not necessarily lead to a catastrophe.

Taking the U.S. Federal Reserve as a model, we will describe our present monetary system in Chapter 4. We will see that it originated with the creation of the Bank of England and has been in existence for three hundred years. We will also discuss in this chapter the meaning of the petrodollar system and the performance of the European Central Bank and that of the central banks of the BRICS countries.

The consequences of having a private elite issue and/or control the money supply will be discussed in Chapter 5.

The benefits of letting the state issue and control the money supply will be seen in Chapter 6.

In Chapter 7 we will describe a solution proposed to solve the problems of our present monetary system. Several solutions for the countries in the European Monetary Union will also be proposed.

We will conclude with an Epilogue in Chapter 8, in which we will analyse the present day situation and summarize the conclusions.

Chapter II

What is Money? Sound and Unsound Fiat Money

Commodity Money

In order to understand the concept of money, let us imagine first that we live in a society in which there are no advanced social institutions, no state. If people living in this society want to trade something, they would probably have to resort to barter. That is, they would interchange goods and services directly. For example, a cow could be traded for a certain amount of grain.

However, after some time, experience shows that certain commodities would be accepted in exchange for everything. This is due to properties such as portability, divisibility and scarcity, among others. These commodities are called money. To be specific, we can define money as some commodity that has the following properties:

1. Store of value.

2. Medium of exchange.

3. Unit of account.

4. Fungibility. Being fungible means that you can trade or substitute it for equal amounts of the same commodity.

Traditionally, gold and silver have been good candidates for money. But, over the course of time, many other commodities (e.g. tobacco, cattle, grain, copper, seashells and tea) at one time or another functioned as money.

According to the previous definition, money is a commodity that facilitates interchanges enormously. This type of money is called commodity money.

Fiat Money

Suppose now that our society has developed socially and we have a state and a certain amount of social institutions such as family, courts, army and government. Paper and printing have been invented too.

In this society, commodity money exists as before, but now it must be subject to law because money is also a social institution, and a very important one. This is why minting is invented and only minted coins are accepted as money, because they have the state's approval. Other forms of money can coexist, but minted coins are the only official money that can be used to pay taxes, for example. As regards the concept of money in a society, Aristotle (384-322 Bc) stated:

"Money exists not by nature but by law."

However, it will not be long before somebody realizes that, instead of carrying money along to make economic transactions, it is better to deposit it in some safekeeping institution and carry a receipt instead. This has the obvious advantages of not having to carry weight and not being exposed to robbery. These receipts start to circulate and they function as money as long as people have confidence in them.

Once the government has seen the benefits of this procedure, it is only a matter of time before it issues its own paper money. This money requires a legal tender law to be accepted by the public and is called fiat money (from Latin, "let it be done", or money by law). Thus, at this stage of society, fiat money is paper money or, more generally, token money that functions as a receipt of some commodity, usually gold. The state guarantees by law that if somebody goes to an appropriate government institution, for example the central bank, he or she can redeem this receipt in gold.

After fiat money is invented, it is evident that we can go one step further and allow fiat money to be a receipt not only of commodities but of goods and services as well. According to this new consideration, the essence of fiat money lies in that it is a receipt of something that has value and, at the same time, it has the state's approval by means of a legal tender law.

Sound and Unsound Fiat Money

The problem with fiat money is that it can be counterfeited and, above all, can be issued in quantities that exceed the value that it represents. This is why we will distinguish between sound and unsound fiat money, the former being fiat money that is backed by commodities or, more generally, goods and services, whereas the latter is not backed by anything valuable.

To emphasize the distinction between the two kinds of fiat money, we can say that, because all goods and services have some human labour incorporated in them, sound fiat money is nothing but a receipt for human labour sanctioned by the state. An obvious example of sound money was the dollar when it was redeemable in gold. We will review some more sophisticated examples of sound fiat money in the next chapter.

On the other hand, unsound fiat money is money created out of nothing, and thus it has no relation whatsoever to human labour. It is only based on the people's confidence in the government. It can be used in economic transactions because legal tender laws compel people to accept it.

The difference between sound and unsound fiat money lies in the value associated to each of them. Sound fiat money gets its value from human labour directly. However, that does not mean that prices should be set by law. For example, if the state determines that one unit of fiat money is equal to a certain amount of gold, it is up to the market to determine what the relative prices of the different goods and services are. Money should play an intermediary role only, facilitating interchanges. The same thing happens in more sophisticated examples, as is the case of the tally sticks, the colonial scrip, the Greenbacks or the MEFO bills, that we will see later in the book. This kind of sound fiat money is introduced into the market by the state in exchange for goods and services, but it is up to the market to determine the relative prices of these. As before, money should only play an intermediary role.

In the case of unsound fiat money however, there is no value attached to it at first. This kind of money gets its value indirectly, usually in a deferred, fraudulent and harmful way. For example, suppose that we live in a society in which fiat money is backed by gold and that a certain amount of fiat money is created out of thin air and is put into circulation. To start with, this is a fraud because there are now more receipts than gold actually exists to back them. But, if this extra money is evenly distributed among the population, as if it were dropped from a helicopter, we would have more money chasing the same goods and services and, therefore, prices would raise. However, they would raise evenly, at the same rate, and everybody would experience this phenomenon at the same time. In this case, nobody would be harmed by the experiment, we would only have a different ratio between fiat money and goods and services. The only problem would be that there is not enough gold to back all fiat money in circulation. If the government changes appropriately in each monetary unit the amount of gold for which it is redeemed, nothing harmful actually occurs.

If, on the other hand, as is usually the case, the extra money created out of nothing is introduced in such a way that only certain influential people receive it first, these people would have an advantage over the rest because when they spend it prices have not gone up yet. But, after some time, when the ordinary people who have not received any extra money at all try to buy something, prices have already raised due to the effect of more money chasing the same goods. Thus, just as a result of this operation, the influential people get benefited because they buy at lower prices and the ordinary people suffer losses in their purchasing power. In addition, one has to consider the fraud that this operation entails, because not all fiat money in circulation is backed by gold. If all of the banks investors go to the central bank to redeem their fiat money in gold, there will be insufficient gold in the vaults to repay them.

As society continues its development, we find ourselves in the present situation in which all money in circulation is unsound fiat money, i.e. money that has been generated out of thin air. It is only the confidence in the government and the legal tender laws that allow this money to be accepted by the people. As mentioned earlier in this section, this kind of money gets its value indirectly and in a delayed and often harmful way. As we will see later in Chapter 4, given our present monetary system, the value of our unsound fiat money comes from the work of the people when the state and the individuals repay their loans and taxes are paid. Under these circumstances, it is the ordinary people who most suffer the consequences of a loss in purchasing power due to price increases, that are an inevitable consequence of the use of unsound money.

The Debt-based Unsound Fiat Money of Today

We will see later in Chapter 4 that all currency in circulation is unsound fiat money created out of nothing and out of debt by the central bank. This central bank happens to be a private bank in the case on the United States, and is called the Federal Reserve. However, it is as "federal" as the Federal Express and has no reserves.

We have not mentioned yet another kind of money that is used today and that happens to be the most important one nowadays. We are referring to money created by commercial banks through fractional reserve banking. The process by which this money is created will be described in detail later in the book. We will content ourselves in this chapter with a brief description of the mechanics of this money creation.

Under fractional reserve banking, commercial banks are required to maintain in their vaults only a fraction, say ten per cent, of the amount that clients have in demand deposits at each bank. The rest of it, ninety per cent, can be lent to other clients. Thus, whenever a bank makes a loan out of this ninety per cent, it is creating money out of thin air through the chequebook that is given to the borrower. This money is either spent or deposited in another bank, where the process starts all over again. In this way, the money supply is exponentially increased out of nothing. Incidentally, this process involves usury, as described in the previous chapter, on the part of the banks. In fact, it is these unearned interest revenues that are responsible for the rampant social inequalities that we observe these days.

To really understand the previous process of money creation, it is very important to realize that people usually think that a demand deposit contract involves the safekeeping by the bank of all the funds deposited because that is what usually happens in other branches of economics. For example, if I deposit a certain amount of chairs in a warehouse, I expect the chairs to remain there until I decide to go and fetch them. However, this is not the case with banks under fractional reserve banking. The process of money creation occurs because the amount of money deposited in the banks is miraculously multiplied through lending, at interest of course, the same money many times. It is to be noticed that this procedure is legal only in the banking system, not in other branches of economics, and constitutes a form of legalized fraud.

Money created by fractional reserve banking is clearly unsound fiat money because it has not been generated out of human labour, it was created out of nothing and out of debt. It is disturbing to know that most of the money in our society today, about 97 per cent, is created in this way.

Another disturbing effect of money creation through fractional reserve banking is that when loans are repaid more money is withdrawn from circulation than it was created. This is because when a loan is returned, we must pay the principal plus the interest. Thus, if we ever pay all our debts, there would be no money left in circulation.

In the next chapter, we will review some examples of successful sound fiat money that have existed in the past.

As mentioned in the previous section, all money created today aquires its value from people's labour when the state and the individuals repay their loans and taxes are paid. Since this money was created out of nothing, it is clear that the process involves a fraud and a tremendous transfer of wealth from ordinary people to a small elite that has done no work to earn the profits involved in this operation.

The money supply under the present monetary system is based upon the amount of currency in circulation plus the deposits in commercial banks. The crucial question, which will be dealt with later in the book, is whether the money supply should be in private or public hands.

The Danger of Money Based On Precious Metals

When the money supply is based on precious metals, typically gold and silver, there are several problems that may appear. Suppose that money is based on gold for simplicity in what follows. What we are about to discuss applies to commodity money, that is coins, as well as to fiat money backed by gold.

The first problem is that there may not be enough gold available to satisfy the needs of the country's economy. In this case, a deflation sets in that may have devastating consequences for this economy. Such was the case of Rome, for example, in the final stages of the Empire, as we will see in Chapter 5.

The second problem is that of a powerful private elite taking control of the money supply through manipulation of the quantity of gold. By restricting the amount of gold, a deflation is generated that may bring the economy to a depression. On the contrary, by allowing too much gold into circulation, an inflation occurs that generates bubbles in the economy. We will provide several examples of these phenomena in Chapter 5.

The Advantages of Sound Fiat Money Issued and Controlled by the State, not Backed by Commodities

The principal advantage of this kind of money is that it can be produced at essentially no cost by the State. For this reason, the State can always issue the quantity of money that the economy requires for an optimal condition. This kind of money is interest and debt free.

The State should be vigilant so that there is no counterfeiting and every monetary unit that is introduced into the economy is backed by human labour. In this case, no inflation should occur. Money would play an intermediary role, facilitating interchanges in the economy. No private elite can manipulate this kind of money if the State adheres to these rules.

We will see several examples of this kind of money in history in Chapter 3. The same pattern always arises, there is no inflation and the economy thrives.

Chapter III

Examples of Sound Fiat Money

In this chapter, we will review some historical examples of the use of sound fiat money not backed by precious metals. The pattern that arises is always the same. When true sound fiat money is used, the economy works efficiently and there is no inflation. However, if the government starts issuing more fiat money than there is backing (a commodity or, more generally, human labour) for it, then inflation sets in and the economy gets into trouble. This last phenomenon usually has its origin in wars for which the government needs more money than actually exists.

Spartan Iron Money

For the first example let's look way back to the foundation of the ancient Spartan way of life originated by its king Lycurgus in 800 BC.

Lycurgus had travelled widely, visiting India, Spain, Libya and the island of Crete. When he returned to Sparta, he took control of the government and established a constitution based on the Cretan model. He took several measures aimed at cleaning up a corrupt society "whose wealth had centred upon a very few", according to Plutarch.

Lycurgus began with a decree that outlawed all gold and silver coinage and declared that all Spartan coins must be made of iron. He let the coin units be of low value and heavy so they were difficult to store and transport. He had the hot iron doused with vinegar to make the metal weak and fragile.

Lycurgus' money was a sound fiat money because the total amount of money in circulation was regulated by law and the value of the symbols serving as money, called Pelanors, depended on limiting the number in circulation.

This monetary system seems to have worked well for three and a half centuries. It was abandoned around 415 BC, after Sparta started a series of campaigns to conquest foreign territories and captured large amounts of gold and silver.

The following quote is from Plutarch's *Lives of Noble Grecians and Romans, Lycurgus chapter*, and gives his reason for the end of this money system.

"For five hundred years, Sparta kept the laws of Lycurgus and was the strongest and most famous city in Greece. But eventually gold and silver were allowed in, and along with them came all of the evils spawned by the love of money. Lysander must take the blame, because he brought home rich spoils from the wars. Although not corrupt himself, Lysander infected Sparta with greed and luxury, and thus subverted the laws of Lycurgus."

Rome Bronze Nomisma

When Numa Pompilius (716-762 BC), Rome's second King, came to power most of the gold and silver that he could use as money was stored away in eastern temple establishments. However, copper was abundant and would be much easier to obtain.

Numa came from Rome's Sabine territory and considered himself a descendant of the Spartans. He was renowned for his high intelligence. He reasoned that if he would institutionalize bronze - an alloy composed of mainly copper, some tin and a bit of lead - as money, the ability of the eastern temples or merchants to control or disrupt Rome's money would be greatly reduced.

Thus, Numa formulated an ingenious plan. He would decree that gold and silver would merely be commodities in his kingdom. They could be traded as unmarked coins or bars, but the real money would be bronze.

This bronze money was clearly a fiat token money. It was called nummi or nomisma at a later point in Numa's reign. Because his name was so close to nummi, some historians think Numa was named after his monetary innovations rather than the money being named after him.

The following quote from Alexander del Mar[1] describes what the Romans had to do in his opinion for the system to function properly or, in our terminology, for the money to be sound fiat money.

> "Therefore, the means necessary to secure and maintain such a money were for the State to monopolize the copper mines, restrict the commerce in copper, strike copper pieces of high artistic merit in order to defeat counterfeiting, stamp them with the mark of the State, render them the sole legal tenders for the payment of domestic contracts, taxes, fines and debts, limit their emission until their value (from universal demand for them and their comparative scarcity) rose to more than that of the metal of which they were composed, and maintain such restriction and over-valuation as the permanent policy of the State. For foreign trade or diplomacy, a supply of gold and silver, coined and uncoined, could be kept in the treasury."

The system worked well, first domestically and then internationally, until the Punic wars with Carthage.

---

1   del Mar, 2000, p. 21

China: The First Fiat Paper Money

China is not only credited with having invented paper but it is also generally recognized to have been the first country in the world to use fiat paper money.

The inspiration for China's paper money actually came from the "white deerskin" money (bai lu pi bi) issued under the reign of Emperor Wu (141-87 BC) of the Han Dynasty, and the "flying money" (fei qian) of the Tang Dynasty (618-907 AD). These were bills of exchange that were traded in private exchanging booths (jufang or jifupu), and in official exchange houses (bianqianwu). In addition to that, textile fabric was also common as a means of payment, as it was part of the tax system. True paper money became a major form of currency during the Northern Song Dynasty (960-1127) with the issuance of the Jiao Zi and Qian Yin, and paper currency then continued under the Southern Song Dynasty (1127-1279) which issued the Hui Zi and Guan Zi.

In ancient China they used iron coins that were circular with a rectangular hole in the middle. Several coins could be strung together in a rope. Merchants soon realized that these strings of coins were too heavy to carry around. It was much more convenient to leave the coins with a trustworthy person and carry a receipt instead. The money could be regained using this receipt. This gave rise to the first fiat paper money, the Jiao Zi.

The Jiao Zi was first issued in 1023 together by 16 merchant princes by order of the Song prefect, Xue Tian, at Chengdu, in the Sichuan Province. This fiat paper money was a piece of paper printed with houses, trees, men and cipher to avoid counterfeiting, and it was sound because it was redeemable in coins. It worked well as long as it remained sound, i.e. backed by an appropriate amount of coins. However, there was eventually a point in time in which the state started issuing more paper money than was covered by coins and prices began to increase.

For this reason, Emperor Huizong (1100-1125) decided in 1105 to replace the Jiao Zi notes by a new fiat paper currency, the Qian Yin. This new paper money, and the subsequent ones, had also problems with inflation because they were not truly sound money[2].

The Tally Sticks

Tally sticks initially served in England as record keeping devices, from at least the twelfth century. But the English tally system originated with King Henry I, son of William the Conqueror, who ascended to the throne in 1100 AD. At that time, taxes were paid directly with goods and services produced by the people. According to the new innovative system, payment was recorded with a piece of wood that had been notched and split in half lengthwise. One half was kept by the treasury and the other by the recipient. Payment could be confirmed by matching the two halves to make sure they "tallied." Given that no stick splits in an even manner and the notches tallying the sums were cut right through both pieces of wood, counterfeiting was virtually impossible.

Tally sticks were in use for 726 years. They were accepted as legal proof in medieval courts and the Napoleonic Code of 1804 still makes reference to the tally stick in Article 1333.

They were used by the government not only as receipts for the payment of taxes but to pay soldiers for their service, farmers for their wheat, and labourers for their labour. At tax time, tallies were accepted by the treasurer in payment of taxes.

It wasn't long before the value of tally sticks in circulation far exceeded gold and silver money. It is estimated that by the end of the seventeenth century the tallies in circulation had a value of about fourteen million pounds, yet the coined metals at the

---

2   More about Chinese paper money can be consulted at Miaozc (2015)

time never exceeded a half million pounds in value. By 1694 the tally sticks evolved into being represented by paper bills and by 1697 they circulated interchangeably as money with banknotes and bank bills.

Tally sticks were a sound fiat money system for the following reasons.

1. They were really bills of exchange, but they were interest free. They were backed by goods and services that did not exist at the time of issue, but would be produced in a short time when taxes were paid. Thus, they could be used like money because they had the King's approval.

2. They were virtually impossible to counterfeit.

3. They could not be produced in unlimited amounts. The number of tallies made would be limited by the estimated production of the people. When the tallies were turned in for taxes, they were retired from the system and new ones had to be created. There could only be an increase in tally sticks if there was a corresponding increase in anticipated production. In this way, inflation was avoided.

Tally sticks are an example of how the government can increase the money supply using sound fiat money when there is no sufficient gold or silver to issue the necessary coins for a prosperous commerce.

Colonial Scrip

The thirteen American Colonies had trouble with England, the home country, over money from the beginning. This is primarily due to the fact that England wanted the colonists to send raw materials back home, but not to trade with each other. In addition, English laws forbade sending coinage to America, while at the same time the Colonies were short of it because they lacked an indigenous supply of gold or silver from which to mint coins. The scant coinage that found its way to the Colonies came from pirates or trade with the Spanish West Indies.

During the period 1632-1692, many agricultural products were legally declared to be money. However, everybody wanted to pay with the least desirable commodities and this caused inefficiencies. Another problem was seen when Virginia and Maryland made tobacco a legal tender in 1633. There was a bumper crop in 1639 and one half of the crop had to be burned to avoid inflation. After some other unsuccessful experiments with different forms of money, the West's first fiat paper money was issued by Massachusetts in 1690 to pay for a military expedition during King William's War. They printed paper bills from copper plates, which were called bills of credit.

The way they were used was that the colonial government first issued bills of credit to pay goods and services and later accepted these bills as payment of taxes, at which time they were retired from circulation.

Soon, other colonial governments followed suit and issued their own bills of credit to serve as a convenient medium of exchange. When they issued too many bills or failed to tax them out of circulation, inflation resulted. This happened especially in New England and the southern Colonies. Pennsylvania, however, controlled the amount of currency in circulation and it remains a prime example in history as a successful fiat paper monetary system. Pennsylvania's fiat paper currency, secured by land, was reported to have generally maintained its value against gold from 1723 until the Revolution broke out in 1775. During this period there was little or no inflation.

Explaining in 1763 to Bank of England directors his ideas on why the colonies were so prosperous, Benjamin Franklin is quoted as saying:

"That is simple. In the Colonies we issue our own money. It is called Colonial Scrip. We issue it in proper proportion to the demands of trade and industry to make the products pass easily from the producers to the consumers. In this manner, creating for ourselves our own paper money, we control its purchasing power, and we have no interest to pay no one"

After Benjamin Franklin gave explanations on the true cause of the prosperity of the Colonies, the Parliament exacted laws forbidding the use of paper money as payment of taxes. This decision brought so many drawbacks and so much poverty to the people in the colonies that it is seen by many as the main cause of the Revolution. The suppression of the Colonial paper money was a much more important factor for the general uprising than the Tea and Stamp Act.

The Greenbacks

Before the Civil War in the United States, the only money issued by the government was gold and silver coins, and only such coins ("specie") were legal tender.

Paper currency in the form of banknotes was issued by privately owned banks, and these notes were redeemable for specie at the bank's office. They were not legal tender, however, and they had value only if the bank was capable of redeeming them. If a bank failed, its notes became worthless.

When the war broke out, neither side had the supplies of gold and silver coin necessary to wage such a challenge.

The Lincoln Administration sought loans from major banks, mostly in New York City. The banks demanded very high interest rates of 24 to 36 percent. Lincoln was outraged, refused to borrow on such terms, and called for other solutions.

The following passage appears in a letter from President Abraham Lincoln to Colonel William F. Elkins.[3] It gives some insight into the feelings that the President may have had with regard to the money powers, as he called them.

"The money powers prey upon the nation in times of peace and conspire against it in times of adversity. The banking powers are more despotic than a monarchy, more insolent than autocracy, more selfish than bureaucracy. They denounce as public enemies all who question their methods or throw light upon their crimes. I have two great enemies, the Southern Army in front of me and the bankers in the rear. Of the two, the one at my rear is my greatest foe."

The solution found by the Lincoln Administration was to bypass the bankers by issuing fiat paper money to pay for the war expenses. A legal tender law was passed on February 25, 1862. Congress at first authorized the Treasury to issue $150 million of so called Greenbacks, with a total of $450 million being put into circulation as the war continued. The Greenbacks were legal tender for all debts public and private, except duties on import and interest on the public debt, which were payable in coin. They were receivable in payment of all loans made to the U.S.

A letter written by President Lincoln to Colonel E D Taylor, considered the father of the Greenbacks, can be found in the Appendix to this book.

The Greenbacks were very difficult to counterfeit because they used a proprietary green chromium tint invented by a Canadian, Dr. Thomas Sterry Hunt, to combat photo duplication. The notes got their name from this "green" ink on their "back". The name did not come from the Lincoln Administration but from the ordinary people, who started calling them Greenbacks.

---

3   The letter is dated November 21, 1864, and was published in Lincoln and Shaw (1950, p. 40), that in turn traces the quote's lineage to Lincoln and Hertz (1931, p. 954)

As regards inflation during the Civil War, the American historian J. G. Randall wrote that "The threat of inflation was more effectively curbed during the Civil War than during the First World War." Also, the American economist John K. Galbraith observed:

> "It is remarkable that without rationing, price controls, or central banking, Chase (the Secretary of the Treasury at the time) could have managed the federal economy so well during the Civil War."

The fact that the Greenbacks were not legal tender for duties on import and interest on the public debt may have been an important negative factor against the currency. In reference to this, the American financial historian Davis R. Dewey wrote:

> "Hence it has been argued that the Greenback circulation issued in 1862 might have kept at par with gold if it, too, had been made receivable for all payments to the Government."

After the war and the assassination of Lincoln, there was a concerted attack of various social groups led by the bankers against the Greenbacks until they were retired from circulation.

The German MEFO Bills

The MEFO bills were a financial instrument created by the National Socialist Government of Germany in 1933 to allow for the activation of the economy, which lay in shambles.

When Adolf Hitler was appointed Chancellor on January 30th, 1933, there were six and a half million people unemployed, there was no gold, and the country was in ruins. To make matters worse, astronomically high war reparations had still to be paid to the victors of World War One.

If the country was to have some economic independence, it could not loan from international banks because this would increase the financial burden even more. Thus, some new monetary device had to be found to get out of the dilemma.

Hitler describes in his book *Mein Kampf* that he once attended a small meeting in which Gottfried Feder's monetary views made a deep impression on him. According to Feder (1883-1941), a former construction engineer turned economist, the money supply should be created and controlled by the state through a nationalized central bank rather than by privately owned banks, to whom interest would have to be paid.

Since Feder's ideas were in principle too innovative and risky, Hitler decided to appoint Hjalmar Schacht, a well-known and experienced German banker at the time, as head of the Reichsbank to carry out a somewhat attenuated version of the monetary reform proposed by Feder.

After denouncing the Treaty of Versailles because the other countries had not met their obligations, the government decided that Germany would create its own sound fiat money, free of debt, through an extensive program of repairs in housing, factories and machines, and through the construction of autobahns.

Hjalmar Schacht himself describes the process in his book *The Magic of Money*: [4]

> "The system worked in the following way: a company with a paid-up capital of one million Marks was formed. A quarter of the capital was subscribed by each of the four firms Siemens, A. G. Gutehoffnungshütte, Rheinstahl and Krupps. Suppliers who fulfilled state orders drew up bills of exchange for their goods, and these bills were accepted by the company. This company was given the registered title

---

4   Schacht, 1967

of Metallforschungsgesellschaft (Metal Research Company, 'MEFO' for short), and for this reason the bills drawn on it were called MEFO bills. The Reich guaranteed all obligations entered into by MEFO, and thus also guaranteed the MEFO bills in full. In essence all the Reichsbank's formal requirements were met by this scheme. It was a question of financing the delivery of goods; MEFO bills were therefore commodity bills. ...

The Reichsbank declared itself ready to prolong the bills, which true to the form laid down were drawn on three months' credit, to a maximum of five years if so required, and this point was new and unusual. Each bill could thus be extended by a further three months, nineteen times running. This was necessary, because the planned economic reconstruction could not be accomplished in three months, but would take a number of years. By and large such extensions by themselves were nothing new with the Reichsbank; it was quite common to prolong agricultural bills, but an extension over five years, together with a firm declaration that such extensions would be granted, that was most unusual. One other aspect was even more unusual. The Reichsbank undertook to accept all MEFO bills at all times, irrespective of their size, number, and due date, and change them into money. The bills were discounted at a uniform rate of four per cent. By these means the MEFO bills were almost given the character of money, and interest-carrying money at that. Banks, savings banks, and firms could hold them in their safes exactly as if they were cash. Over and above this they proved to be the best of all interest-bearing liquid investments, in contrast to long-dated securities. In all, MEFO bill credit transactions took place over a period of four years, and had by 1938 reached a total volume of twelve billion Marks."

The Reichsbank officials were entrusted with the task of examining all bills to ensure that they were issued only against deliveries of goods, and not for any other purposes. Bills which did not meet this requirement were rejected. Thus, the MEFO bills acted like sound fiat money and were non-inflationary because they were backed by human labour.

The following words are part of a speech given by Hitler on February 20th, 1938, in which he addresses the question of the role of money in Germany at the time. (A more extensive part of this speech is given in English in the Appendix to this book.)

"It will also be our task in the future to warn the German people against all kinds of illusions. The worst illusion is to think that one can enjoy something in life that has not been previously created and produced.

It will also be our duty in the future to make clear to all German people, in the city as well as in the land, that the value of their labour is and should always be equal to their salary.

That is, the countryman can only receive for his products what the man in the city has previously produced, and the man in the city can only get what the countryman has previously obtained from his land, and all of them can only make interchanges while they are producing, and money can only play an intermediary role in this process.

Money cannot have an intrinsic value. Each new Mark that is paid in Germany presupposes an additional human labour valued one Mark. Otherwise, this Mark is an empty piece of paper that has no purchasing power.

We want however our Reichsmark to be an honourable banknote, an honourable receipt for the result of an equally honourable human labour.

This is the only real and authentic backing of a currency. In this way we have made it possible, without gold and foreign currencies, to keep the value of the German Mark stable, and we have also kept our savings stable, in times in which those countries that were swimming in gold and foreign currencies had to devalue their currencies."

After two years of using this sound fiat money, unemployment had almost disappeared and in five years Germany was the greatest economic power in the European continent. The situation in Germany during the period 1933-1939 should be compared with that of the United States during the same period, which were mired in a depression and only got out of it when the events of World War Two forced them to mobilize the economy for the war effort.

Some historians have maintained that the economic success of Germany in the years 1933-1939 was primarily due to defence spending. However, the following table shows that this is not the case.

Year	Defence Expenditure RM	National Income
1933/34	1.9 billion	4%
1934/35	1.9 billion	4%
1935/36	4.0 billion	7%
1936/37	5.8 billion	9%
1937/38	8.2 billion	11%
1938/39	18.4 billion	22%

Chapter IV

Fraud, Inefficiency and Deception

The Bank of England

Our present monetary system has its roots in the creation of the Bank of England in 1694. The whole scheme was brought into existence because England was in financial ruin by the end of the 1600s after fifty years of more or less continuous wars with France and sometimes the Netherlands and desperately needed money to pursue her political purpose.

But the main reason for the establishment of the Bank of England was that the military campaign of Prince William of Orange to dethrone King James II was financed by Money Lenders from Amsterdam, who had been practising usury (in the sense of this book) for a long time. In return for their support, William III (1689-1702) would yield to their demands and would surrender the royal prerogative of issuing England's money, free of debt and interest, to a privately owned central bank.

London at the time had many independent unregulated goldsmiths and bankers who were allowed to mint the coins of the realm at the Royal Mint, and the money market was chaotic with varying rates of exchange. The goldsmiths were charging 30 to 80 per cent yearly on small loans and were very unpopular for their greed and anti-social behaviour. For this reason, a lot of people demanded a bank to regulate the currency and to lower interest rates. What they didn't suspect was that the solution would be one of the biggest scams in the history of mankind.

The project of founding a privately owned central bank

originated with an allegedly retired buccaneer, the Scot William Paterson[1], who wrote a pamphlet in 1693 titled *A brief Account of the Intended Bank of England*. He is quoted as saying that:

> "The bank hath benefit of interest on all moneys which it creates out of nothing."

Frantic government officials met with the money lenders, who had arrived from Amsterdam surrounding Prince William of Orange, to beg for the loans necessary to pursue their political ends. As suggested by Paterson's proposal, the price was high: a government sanctioned, privately owned central bank, which could issue money created out of nothing as loans.

The bill for the establishment of the Bank of England was debated in July 1694, at the precise moment in summer in which most of the rural members of the House of Commons were taking care of their summer tasks and harvesting their crops. It was passed in stealth, as a rider to a tax bill on shipping tonnage.

The Bank of England was to be the modern world's first privately owned national central bank in a powerful country, though earlier deposit banks had existed in Venice (1361), Amsterdam (1609), and Sweden (1661), which issued the first bank notes in Europe that same year, 1661. Although it was deceptively called the Bank of England to make the general population think it was part of the government, it was not. Like any other private corporation, the Bank of England sold shares to get started.

The investors, whose names were never revealed, were supposed to put up one and a quarter million British pounds in gold coin to buy their shares in the Bank. But only £750,000 pounds was ever received. Despite that, the Bank of England was duly chartered in 1694, and started out in the business of loaning out several times the money it supposedly had in reserves, all at interest.

---

1   Andréadès, 1966, p. 60

In exchange, the new bank would loan British Crown as much as it wanted. The debt was secured by direct taxation of the British people. So, legalization of the Bank of England mounted to nothing less than legalized counterfeiting of a national currency for private gain based on usury, as defined in the Introduction to this book.

As we will see in the next section, in which we will describe the process in detail, the central bank scam is really a hidden tax, but one that benefits private banks more than the government. We will use the central bank of the United States, the Federal Reserve, as a model to illustrate the whole scheme because this central bank is the most important one in the world. The process has several stages.

The Federal Reserve: How the System Works

From the birth of the United States in 1783 until 1913, there was a struggle between the politicians and the bankers for the establishment of a central bank. The bankers managed to convince the politicians on three occasions to create a central bank, but on each occasion the bank was closed after some time. However, the bankers finally succeeded when the Federal Reserve Act was signed into law by President Woodrow Wilson at 6:02 p.m., December 23rd, 1913, after many Senators and Representatives had left Washington for the Holidays, having been assured by the leadership that nothing would be done until long after the Christmas recess. Only weeks earlier, Congress had passed a bill legalizing income tax.

The Federal Reserve (Fed) is a privately owned bank that has shareholders but no reserves. Thus, the Federal Reserve is about as federal as Federal Express. Income tax is the method devised by the Fed owners to ensure that the government returns the principal plus interest of all the loans created out of nothing that are made to it by the bank.

The present monetary system of most countries is similar to that of the United States. Since the Federal Reserve is the most important central bank in the world, we will describe in this section how the monetary system works in the United States today.

STAGE I

Creation of Base Money Through the Fed

Whenever the Government wants money, for example to pay for some electoral promises, the Treasury issues some bonds that are offered for bid at an auction. When these bonds are bought by commercial banks, the Government gets the money it desires. The banks can get money in turn by selling Treasury bonds to the Fed through so called "open market operations". The Fed pays for the bonds by writing a check that has no deposits to back it, so that it is in fact creating money out of nothing in exchange for the bonds.

The whole process can be seen as the Government swapping bonds for money created out of nothing between the Treasury and the Fed, with the commercial banks as intermediaries. In this way, the so called "Base Money" is created. It is to be noticed that all this money is created out of debt and out of nothing and that in each step of the previous procedure the commercial banks make a profit. This amounts to legalized counterfeiting on the part of the Fed.

Compare this situation to that in which there is a state bank instead of a privately owned central bank. In this case, money is created directly by the Treasury, interest free, and given to the Government to spend on infrastructure, housing, etc. The role of the state bank in this scenario is to remain alert and to ensure that the money is correctly spent. In this way, inflation is prevented, no national debt is generated, and the money plays only an intermediary role. The money so created is sound fiat money because it has been issued by the Treasury and is backed by human labour. Also, in this situation commercial banks are not allowed to create money through fractional reserve banking. That is, it is required that commercial banks keep a 100 per cent reserve ratio on their deposits. All money deposited with them is kept in their vaults, thus fulfilling the safekeeping function that people erroneously believe that they do now. The banks can of course make loans, but the funds for this function must be collected from time deposits, shares or debentures.

STAGE II

Creation of Money Through Fractional Reserve Banking

With the money obtained in Stage I, the Government pays for social programs, public works, army, etc. The people who receive this money from the Government deposit it in commercial banks and here is where the most important part of the money creation process gets started. Instead of keeping the deposits in their vaults from which they can make loans, as many people think they do, the banks hold only a fraction, say 10 per cent, and lend the other 90% out as loans despite not having the deposits in their vaults to cover them. This is of course a form of legalized fraud. The same sort of behaviour would be considered a crime in other branches of economics.

Thus, if I deposit for example 100 dollars in a bank, the bank keeps 10 dollars in the vault available for withdrawal and lends out the other 90 dollars to other customers. By this process, the bank creates 90 dollars out of nothing because it gives each borrower a chequebook. In this way, the original 100 dollars are turned into 190 dollars.

The borrowers buy something with the 90 dollars and the people who receive this money, the sellers, deposit these 90 dollars in turn in other banks. This money is re-lent and re-deposited several times so that the original 100 dollars become 1000 dollars in a sort of miraculous way. Here are the mathematics. If r=.1 and x=100, then

$$x + x(1 - r) + x(1 + x)^2 + x(1 + x)^3 + \cdots = x\frac{1}{1 - (1 - r)} = 1000$$

Thus, in the previous example the initial deposit is expanded by a factor of 10. In general, it is expanded by a factor of 1/r, where r is the so called "reserve ratio", i.e. the fraction of the deposits that commercial banks have to hold in their vaults in case people want to withdraw some money from the bank.

The money supply is defined as the currency in circulation plus the deposits in commercial banks.

At this stage, it is evident that the money supply is unsound fiat money because it has been generated without taking into account any human labour that might have been used to back it. Not only that, it is also clear that this process of money creation involves usury as we defined it in the Introduction to this book because a profit is obtained from money that is created out of thin air. The question then arises as to what is the relationship between the money supply and the human labour used in the economy. In other words, what is the value of the money created by the present monetary system? This point is addressed in the next stage.

STAGE III

Repayment of Loans and Taxation

Before the Fed was established in 1913, a law had been passed a few weeks earlier that same year in which income tax was introduced. The reason for this law was to make sure that the loans made by the Fed to the Government would be repaid. And this is exactly what happens today. The taxes that people pay to the IRS (Internal Revenue Service) are used, among other things, to pay the Fed the principal plus the interest of the money that it creates out of thin air for loans to the Government. However, this tax money has the value incorporated through the human labour used to generate it, whereas the checks drawn by the Fed are based on nothing and have therefore no intrinsic value.

It is to be noticed that since the Fed is a private bank, it has shareholders, many of whom are foreigners. Thus, taxes are also used to pay these shareholders a dividend each year, which happens to be 6 per cent. We will give a list of some of these foreign shareholders at the end of this section.

At the same time, people have to work to repay the loans made by commercial banks to private individuals, and it is to be further noticed that most of these loans are made out of money that is created out of thin air through fractional reserve banking. For this reason, the usurious present monetary system forces the people to pay the bankers several times for something that has no intrinsic value. The system implies thus a great transfer of wealth from private individuals to the bankers, who earn these profits without having worked for them. Some consequences of this process are addressed in the next stage.

STAGE IV

National Debt and Inflation

The present monetary system implies that each dollar in the money supply is based on debt. That is, if there is one dollar only for example, we have to return this dollar plus the interest. Assuming the interest is also one dollar, there is no money to repay the loan. In order to repay it, we have to borrow another dollar into existence, in which case we would have two dollars in the money supply and four dollars in debt. If we continue this process, we would end up with some quantity in the money supply and a double quantity in debt. If we would extinguish the debt, there would be no money in the money supply. Thus, the amount of debt in the economy cannot be extinguished, it has to grow forever by the very design of the system.

The National Debt cannot have a Debt Ceiling. Imposing a debt ceiling is nonsense because we would have deflation and eventually no money. For this reason, the Government cannot act as a responsible family, it cannot balance spending and income. The whole procedure of money creation is a scam designed to rob the people. Hence the persistent mantra that growth must be maintained at all costs. Because if all loans were to be repaid, the money supply would vanish. One manifestation of this phenomenon is programmed obsolescence, a business strategy in which the obsolescence of a product is planned and built into it from its conception. The purpose of this is that in future the consumer feels a need to purchase new products and services that the manufacturer brings out as replacements for the old ones. Another consequence of the growth syndrome is the partial de-industrialization of the developed world so that inferior goods have to be continually produced by third world countries in order to fuel this growth syndrome.

Another mechanism of institutionalized theft is that of inflation. Since all money in the money supply has been created without any consideration to human labour or commodity backing, it can come as no surprise that inflation is often generated. The process is as follows. In a context of low interest rates arbitrarily fixed by the Fed, the Government and the commercial banks introduce excess money into the economy little by little, starting with the people and the institutions that have more influence on the power elite. These people have an advantage with respect to ordinary people because when they start spending the new unbacked money prices have not gone up yet. But, after some time, because more money chasing the same goods causes prices to raise, when the ordinary people spend their money prices have already risen and they lose purchasing power.

Thus, inflation acts as a hidden tax on ordinary people. Politicians can spend more trying to be more popular at the expense of people being robbed by inflation over time.

Don't worry if you don't understand how the monetary system works at first. As we said in the Introduction to this book, the famous British economist John Maynard Keynes, referring to the monetary system, wrote in *The Economic Consequences of the Peace*[2] that:

> "By this means the government may secretly and unobserved, confiscate the wealth of the people, and not one man in a million will detect the theft."

The Federal Reserve Shareholders

Since its inauguration in 1913, the Federal Reserve has operated solely as a private bank for the benefit of private bankers. According to E. Mullins in his book *The Secrets of the Federal Reserve*:[3]

> "The shareholders of these banks which own the stock of the Federal Reserve Bank of New York are the people who have controlled our political and economic destinies since 1914. They are:

- The Rothschild family, of Europe
- Lazard Freres (Eugene Meyer)
- Kuhn Loeb Company
- Warburg Company
- Lehman Brothers
- Goldman Sachs
- The Rockefeller family
- J.P. Morgan interests

---

2   Keynes, 1920

3   Mullins, 1983

These interests have merged and consolidated in recent years, so that the control is much more concentrated. National Bank of Commerce is now Morgan Guaranty Trust Company. Lehman Brothers has merged with Kuhn, Loeb Company, First National Bank has merged with the National City Bank, and in the other eleven Federal Reserve Districts, these same shareholders indirectly own or control shares in those banks, with the other shares owned by the leading families in those areas who own or control the principal industries in these regions."

The US Dollar as Reserve Currency: The Petrodollar System

To understand the role of the U.S. dollar in the world since World War Two, let us begin by considering the following excerpt of an article by Jerry Robinson titled *Preparing for the Collapse of the Petrodollar System, Part 2*.[4]

"In the early 1970s, the final vestiges of the international gold-backed dollar standard, known as the Bretton Woods arrangement, had collapsed. Many foreign nations who had previously agreed to a gold-backed dollar as the global reserve currency were now having serious mixed feelings about the arrangement. Nations like Britain, France, and Germany determined that a cash-strapped and debt-crazed United States was in no financial shape to be leading the global economy. These were just a few of the many nations which began demanding gold in exchange for their dollars.

Despite pressure from foreign nations to protect the dollar's value by reining in excessive government spending, Washington displayed little fiscal constraint and continued to live far beyond its means. It had become obvious to all that America lacked the basic fiscal discipline which could prevent the destruction of its own currency.

---

4   Robinson, 2012a

Like previous governments before it, America had figured out how to "game" the global reserve currency system for its own benefit, leaving foreign nations in an economically vulnerable position. After America and its citizens had tasted the sweet fruit of excessive living at the expense of other nations, the party was over.

It is unfair, however, to say that the Washington elites were blind to the deep economic issues confronting it in the late 1960's and early 1970's. Washington knew that the "dollars for gold" had become completely unsustainable. But instead of seeking solutions to the global economic imbalances that had been created by America's excessive deficits, Washington's primary concern was how to gain an even greater stranglehold on the global economy.

In order to ensure their economic hegemony, and thereby preserve an increasing demand for the dollar, the Washington elites needed a plan. In order for this plan to succeed, it would require that the artificial dollar demand that had been lost in the wake of the Bretton Woods collapse be replaced through some other mechanism.

According to John Perkins, the author of Confessions of an Economic Hit Man: The Shocking Story of How America Really Took Over the World, that plan came in the form of the petrodollar system...

But what exactly is the petrodollar system? First, let's define what a petrodollar is.

A petrodollar is a U.S. dollar that is received by an oil producer in exchange for selling oil, and that is then deposited into Western banks.

Despite the seeming simplicity of this arrangement of "dollars for oil," the petrodollar system is actually highly complex and one with many moving parts. It is this complexity that prevents the petrodollar system from being properly understood by the American public.

Allow me to provide a very basic overview regarding the history and the mechanics of the petrodollar system. It is my belief that once you understand this "dollars for oil" arrangement, you will gain a more accurate understanding of what motivates America's economic (and especially foreign) policy.

So, let's take a closer look...

The Rise of the Petrodollar System

The petrodollar system originated in the early 1970s in the wake of the Bretton Woods collapse.

President Richard M. Nixon and his globalist sidekick, Secretary of State, Henry Kissinger, knew that their destruction of the international gold standard under the Bretton Woods arrangement would cause a decline in the artificial global demand for the U.S. dollar. Maintaining this "artificial dollar demand" was vital if the United States were to continue expanding its "welfare and warfare" spending.

In a series of meetings, the United States — represented by then U.S. Secretary of State Henry Kissinger — and the Saudi royal family made a powerful agreement. (Several authors have worked to compile data on the origins of the petrodollar system, some exhaustively, including Richard Duncan, William R. Clark, David E. Spiro, Charles Goyette and F. William Engdahl).

According to the agreement, the United States would offer military protection for Saudi Arabia's oil fields. The U.S. also agreed to provide the Saudis with weapons, and perhaps most importantly, guaranteed protection from Israel.

The Saudi royal family knew a good deal when they saw one. They were more than happy to accept American weapons and a U.S. guarantee to restrain attacks from neighbouring Israel.

Naturally, the Saudis wondered how much all of this U.S. military muscle was going to cost...

What exactly did the United States want in exchange for their weapons and military protection?

The Americans laid out their terms. They were simple and two-fold.

1) The Saudis must agree to price all of their oil sales in U.S. dollars only. (In other words, the Saudis were to refuse all other currencies except the U.S. dollar as payment for their oil exports.)

2) The Saudis would be open to investing their surplus oil proceeds in U.S. debt securities.

You can almost hear one of the Saudi officials in a meeting saying: "Really? That's all? You don't want any of our money or our oil? You just want to tell us how to price our oil and then you will give us weapons, military support, and guaranteed protection from our enemy, Israel? You've got a deal!"

However, the U.S. had done its economic homework. If they could get the Saudis to buy into this deal, it would be enough to launch them into the economic stratosphere in the coming decades.

Fast forward to 1974 when the petrodollar system was fully operational in Saudi Arabia. And just as the United States had cleverly calculated, it did not take long before other oil-producing nations wanted in on the deal.

By 1975, all of the oil-producing nations of OPEC had agreed to price their oil in dollars and to hold their surplus oil proceeds in U.S. government debt securities in exchange for the generous offers by the U.S. Just dangle weapons, military aid, and guaranteed protection from Israel in front of third world, oil-rich, Middle East nations... and let the bidding begin.

Nixon and Kissinger had successfully bridged the gap between the failed Bretton Woods arrangement and the new Petrodollar system. The global artificial demand for U.S. dollars would not only remain intact, it would soar due to the increasing demand for oil around the world.

And from the perspective of empire, this new "dollars for oil" system was much more preferred over the former "dollars for gold" system as its economic requirements were much less stringent. Without the constraints imposed by a rigid gold standard, the U.S. monetary base could be grown at exponential rates.

It should come as no surprise that the United States maintains a major military presence in much of the Persian Gulf region, including the following countries: Bahrain, Iraq, Kuwait, Oman, Qatar, Saudi Arabia, United Arab Emirates, Egypt, Israel, Jordan, and Yemen. The truth is easy to find when you follow the money..."

To understand the role played by the Eurasian region in the Petrodollar system, we present the following excerpt taken from the article by Jerry Robinson titled *Preparing for the Collapse of the Petrodollar System, Part 4:*[5]

---

5   Robinson, 2012b

"Additionally, the news of Afghanistan's tremendous mineral wealth, and the vast oil and natural gas reserves of nearby countries, was published for all to read in a 1997 book by globalist Zbigniew Brzezinski entitled *The Grand Chessboard: American Primacy and Its Geostrategic Imperatives*.[6]

Brzezinski, who is a former Presidential advisor and a member of both the Bilderbergers and the Council on Foreign Relations, states in his book what was commonly known among the global elites in the mid-1990's about the importance of the Central Asian region:

"*...the Eurasian Balkans are infinitely more important as a potential economic prize: an enormous concentration of natural gas and oil reserves is located in the region, in addition to important minerals, including gold.*"[7]

Brzezinski continues:

"*America's global primacy is directly dependent on how long and how effectively its preponderance on the Eurasian continent is sustained... A power that dominates Eurasia would control two of the world's three most advanced and economically productive regions... most of the world's physical wealth is there as well, both in its enterprises and underneath its soil.*"[8]

In addition to the vast mineral wealth, which the United States Geological Survey reported as early as 2007 — three years before it released its "bogus finding" to the mainstream press as a legitimate news story — Central Asia is also extremely rich in oil and natural gas.

According to the BP Statistical Review 2011, Kazakhstan had the ninth largest proven oil reserves in the world with

---

6   Brzezinski, 1997

7   Page 124

8   Pages 30-31

well over 30 billion barrels. This is larger than China (25.6 billion barrels), Qatar (25.3 billion) and Brazil (12.9 billion).

What Russia and Britain both failed to do in previous decades during the Great Game, America appears willing and able to do. However, America will face formidable opposition and competition for these same resources from the Russians and especially the Chinese. Again, Brzezinski points out the obvious when he writes: *"China's growing economic presence in the region and its political stake in the area's independence are also congruent with America's interests."* [9]

In order to successfully conquer the region of Central Asia, Brzezinski writes that the West must seek to:

"prevent collusion and maintain security dependence among the vassals, to keep tributaries pliant and protected, and to keep the barbarians from coming together." [10]

I cannot think of a better description of what the U.S.-led wars in the region have created than this last sentence.

How do you "prevent collusion and maintain security dependence?" By keeping the region in a perpetual state of war and upheaval. This is the classic "divide and conquer" strategy that Western nations have employed in the resource-rich regions for centuries. But the American empire deserves credit for cleverly disguising its true intentions in its conquests by appealing to a bogus "war on terror" along with its relationship with Israel. By creating an enemy figure in the form of "global terrorism" along with whipping up national "support" for Israel, the U.S. has made it easy for the public to turn a blind eye towards the nation's aggressive foreign policy in most parts of the world. In fact, it appears that some Americans actually believe that the bankrupt U.S. Empire has pure intentions in conquests. However, this fantasy of America

---

9   Page 148

10   Page 40

being guided by its better angels in all things related to foreign policy entraps only the weakest of minds."

The European Central Bank

The justification for the existence of the European Central Bank (ECB) is given in the Bank's web page[11], where you can read:

"A central bank is a public institution that manages the currency of a country or group of countries and controls the money supply – literally, the amount of money in circulation. The main objective of many central banks is price stability. In some countries, central banks are also required by law to act in support of full employment.

One of the main tools of any central bank is setting interest rates – the "cost of money" – as part of its monetary policy. A central bank is not a commercial bank. An individual cannot open an account at a central bank or ask it for a loan and, as a public body, it is not motivated by profit.

It does act as a bank for the commercial banks and this is how it influences the flow of money and credit in the economy to achieve stable prices. Commercial banks can turn to a central bank to borrow money, usually to cover very short-term needs. To borrow from the central bank they have to give collateral – an asset like a government bond or a corporate bond that has a value and acts as a guarantee that they will repay the money.

Because commercial banks might lend long-term against short-term deposits, they can face "liquidity" problems – a situation where they have the money to repay a debt but not the ability to turn it into cash quickly. This is where a central bank can step in as a "lender of last resort." This helps keep

---

11   http://www.ecb.europa.eu/explainers/tell-me/html/what-is-a-central-bank.en.html

the financial system stable. Central banks can have a wide range of tasks besides monetary policy. They usually issue banknotes and coins, often ensure the smooth functioning of payment systems for banks and traded financial instruments, manage foreign reserves, and play a role in informing the public about the economy. Many central banks also contribute to the stability of the financial system by supervising the commercial banks to make sure the lenders are not taking too many risks."

The main difference with respect to the Federal Reserve of the United States is that the ECB is not a private bank. In theory, the ECB should look after the interests of its citizens and not after those of a private elite, although most of the money supply continues to be generated by commercial banks in a way similar to that of the United States. However, this has not been the case, as the behaviour of the ECB showed during the banking crisis of 2008. In the years prior to the crisis, the ECB followed suit in almost all of the initiatives that the Fed had taken in the United States, thus promoting the same disastrous consequences in Europe.

Prior to the creation of the Euro, the Deutschmark had a reputation of being a very solid currency, even competing with the dollar. This was seen by several European countries, above all France, as something embarrassing because it highlighted the weaknesses of the other European currencies. The behaviour of the Bundesbank forced other European countries to try to follow suit if they did not want to be criticized for their lax monetary policy. We can say that the Bundesbank was a more independent central bank that indeed cared more for its citizens than other European central banks.

When the Berlin Wall fell in 1989, the prospect of German Reunification arose fears in France and the U.K. that Germany could become too powerful again. As explained in the article *Germany was strong-armed by French into swapping the*

Deutschmark for the Euro by Allan Hall in the *Mail Online*[12], the price for German Reunification was the abandonment of the Deutschmark and the creation of a new European currency, the Euro. In this way, the strict policies of the Bundesbank would be abandoned and the new central bank, the ECB, would be much more susceptible to political manipulation. And this is exactly what happened. Here is an excerpt of the previous article:

"Francois Mitterand, the French president from 1981 to 1995, knew his neighbours were more than reluctant to trade one of the world's strongest currencies - administered by an equally strong central bank - for an unknown quantity.

Der Spiegel cites the minutes of discussions it has seen between Mitterand and the then German foreign minister Hans-Dietrich Genscher in the late 1980s and early 1990s as proof of a secret pact to dump the mark as the price of re-making a single nation."

The Bank for International Settlements

One can read in the Bank's web page:[13]

"The Bank for International Settlements (BIS) was established in 1930 in Basel, Switzerland. It is an international organisation, created pursuant to an international treaty (The Hague Agreements of 1930). Its shareholding members are central banks and monetary authorities.

The mission of the BIS is to serve central banks in their pursuit of monetary and financial stability, to foster international cooperation in those areas and to act as a bank for central banks."

---

12   Hall, 2010

13   https://www.bis.org/about/history.htm

However, more insight as to the true nature of the BIS was provided by Professor Carroll Quigley of Georgetown University, who wrote in his book *Tragedy and Hope: A History of the World in Our Time:*[14],

"In addition to these pragmatic goals, the powers of financial capitalism had another far-reaching aim, nothing less than to create a world system of financial control in private hands able to dominate the political system of each country and the economy of the world as a whole. This system was to be controlled in feudalist fashion by the central banks of the world acting in concert, by secret agreements arrived at in frequent private meetings and conferences. The apex of the system was to be the Bank of International Settlements in Basle, Switzerland, a private bank owned and controlled by the world's central banks which were themselves private corporations. Each central bank, in the hands of men like Montagu Norman of the Bank of England, Benjamin Strong of the New York Federal Reserve Bank, Charles Rist of the Bank of France, and Hjalmar Schacht of the Reichsbank, sought to dominate its government by its ability to control Treasury loans, to manipulate foreign exchanges, to influence the level of economic activity in the country, and to influence cooperative politicians by subsequent economic rewards in the business world."

---

14   Quigley, 1966, p. 324

Chapter V

Money Supply in Private Hands

The monetary historian Alexander Del Mar in *History of Monetary Systems* [1] wrote:

> "As a rule political economists do not take the trouble to study the history of money; it is much easier to imagine it and to deduce the principles of this imaginary knowledge."

Should the money supply be in private or public hands? In this chapter, we will show how easily one can manipulate the money supply if it is issued and controlled by a private elite. The consequences of this manipulation are disastrous, as we will see.

When private bankers take control of the money creation process, there are recurring cycles of prosperity and poverty, embedded inflation, unemployment, wars, and an enormous and increasing transfer of wealth and political power to a tiny clique who control politicians, mainstream media and cinema, dictates the main trends in academia, and decides the course of geopolitics in the country.

On the contrary, we will show in the next chapter that things are very different if the money supply is in the hands of the state. In this case, there are numerous examples in history that show that there is peace and prosperity, there are few inequalities, and there is no inflation.

---

1   del Mar, 2000

Intentionally Generated Deflations and Inflations

In this section, we will provide several examples in history of deflations and inflations that were originated by a power elite by manipulating the money supply.

The Fall of the Roman Empire

Jaromir Benes and Michael Kumhof stated on p. 14 of *The Chicago Plan Revisited*[2], that:

> "Many historians (Del Mar, 1895) have partly attributed the eventual collapse of the Roman republic to the emergence of a plutocracy that accumulated immense private wealth at the expense of the general citizenry. Their ascendancy was facilitated by the introduction of privately controlled silver money, and later gold money, at prices that far exceeded their earlier commodity value prices, during the emergency period of the Punic wars."

In fact, as Stephen Zarlenga in his book *Lost Science of Money*[3] put it:

> "The combined evidence on wealth concentration, the absence of mining, the normal erosion of the coinage through usage and the tendency of precious metals - especially silver - to flow eastward, presents a powerful argument that an inadequate supply of circulating medium – of money – was a (the?) major factor in the continued decline in the Roman Empire.
>
> Behind that scarcity, ultimately, was a huge error in monetary theory, that some ideologues still make today - the false belief

---

2   Benes and Kumhof, 2012

3   Zarlenga, 2002, p. 100

that money should be a commodity or economic good; that is, wealth rather than a legally based abstract power."

Tulipmania

The term Tulipmania refers to the seventeenth century Dutch speculative mania that caused explosive increases in the price of tulip bulbs. According to monetary historian Alexander Del Mar in *History of Monetary Systems*[4], this phenomenon was caused by the tremendous increase of the quantity of precious metals that took place in Holland as a result of the free coinage law of the revolutionary government. Del Mar wrote:

"Under the private coinage law of the republic, the bank of Amsterdam, a private institution, received deposits of any kind of silver coins, giving credit only for the fine metal contained in them, and measuring its value in sols banco of twenty to the Dutch florin. Its payments were made upon the same basis. The bank also received gold coins on deposit, valuing them (in sols banco) at what they actually fetched in the mart of Amsterdam. This custom deprived the gold and silver coins of Holland of such part of their value as they had previously derived from royal seal, proclamation and seigniorage..."

"Indeed, it destroyed money altogether; it made a market value for the precious metals, a thing hitherto unknown; it practically established unlimited coinage, and thus substituted metal, in place of money, as the measure of value..."

"Under the stimulus of "free" coinage, an immense quantity of precious metals now found their way to Holland, and a local rise of prices ensued, which found one form of expression in the curious mania of buying tulips at prices often exceeding that of the ground on which they were grown..."

---

4   del Mar, 2000, pp. 324-326

"In 1648, when the Peace of Westphalia acknowledged the independence of the Dutch republic, the latter stopped the "free" coinage of silver florins and only permitted it for gold ducats, which in Holland had no legal value. This legislation discouraged the imports of silver bullion, checked the rise of prices, and put an end to the tulip mania."

The First Bank of the United States

The first *de facto* central bank of the United States, the Bank of North America, opened in Philadelphia on January 7, 1782, before the end of the War of Independence on September 3, 1783. It was followed by a second central bank, the First Bank of the United States that was chartered for a term of twenty years by the United States Congress on February 25, 1791. The new bank started with an initial capitalization of $10 million, $2 million of which was owned by the government and the remaining $8 million by private investors. The size of its capitalization made the Bank not only the largest financial institution, but the largest corporation of any type in the new nation.

The bank had been proposed by George Washington's Secretary of the Treasury, Alexander Hamilton, using the charter of the Bank of England as the basis for his plan. However, Hamilton's bank proposal faced widespread resistance from Secretary of State Thomas Jefferson and future president James Madison. Jefferson and Madison also opposed a second of the three proposals of Hamilton, establishing an official government Mint. In fact, Jefferson would later write in a letter to John Taylor in 1816:

"And I sincerely believe with you, that banking establishments are more dangerous than standing armies; & that the principle of spending money to be paid by posterity, under the name of funding, is but swindling futurity on a large scale."

Ultimately, whether because of or in spite of the bill's opponents, on April 25, 1791, Washington signed the "bank bill" into law.

In the year 1792, William Duer, the assistant secretary of the treasury, and Alexander Macomb, an American merchant, speculated against stock held by the Bank of New York. In the background, the First Bank of the United States engaged in a large credit expansion and so fuelled the wave of speculation. This led to the first crash in the history of the United States known as the "Panic of 1792". By flooding the market with its discounts (loans) and banknotes and then sharply reversing course and calling in many of the loans, the bank caused the very first U.S. securities market crash by forcing speculators to sell their stocks.

After Hamilton left office in 1795, the new Secretary of the Treasury, Oliver Wolcott Jr., informed Congress that more money was needed by the government. He advised selling the government's shares of stock in the Bank and Congress quickly agreed. The sales began in 1796 and ended in 1802. In this way, the bank became completely privately owned, with three-fourths of the ownership of the stock being held by foreigners.

The bank's charter expired in 1811 under President James Madison. According to R.E. Search in his book *Lincoln Money Martyred*[5]:

> "In 1809 a bill was put before Congress to renew its charter, which was to expire two years later. The debate in Congress on this bill was very heated, and the State Legislatures in both Pennsylvania and Virginia passed resolutions memorializing the National Congress to prevent its passage. History tells us that Thomas Jefferson was violently opposed to the renewal bill."

> "... The newspapers of that time are quoted as calling the bank bill "A great swindle," and in other places referring to the bank as "A vulture," "A viper," and "A cobra" "

---

5   Search, 1989

Finally, the bill to re-charter failed in the House of Representatives by one vote, 65 to 64, on January 24, 1811, and the bank was closed on March 3, 1811.

The Second Bank of the United States

Shortly before the U.S. Congress decided not to renew the charter of the First Bank of the United States, Nathan Rothschild, who had lent money to the U.S. Government and certain states and was a great supporter of the bank, is reported to have threatened "Either the application for renewal of the Charter is granted or the United States will find itself involved in a most disastrous war."

Whether this story is true or not, the fact is that there was finally war between the U.S. and England, the War of 1812. When hostilities ended in 1814, 24,000 lives had been lost and the U.S. was in great financial difficulty. As a consequence of this, the Second Bank of the United States was established on August 24, 1816. Thus, it seems that the international bankers were the only ones who benefited from that war.

Sometime later in 1832, Andrew Jackson would say about the Second Bank of the United States: [6]

> "You are a den of vipers. I intend to rout you out and by the Eternal God I will rout you out. If the people only understood the rank injustice of our money and banking system, there would be a revolution before morning."

In February 1836, the bank became a private corporation under Pennsylvania commonwealth law. A shortage of hard currency ensued, causing the Panic of 1837 and lasting approximately seven years. The Bank suspended payment in 1839 and was liquidated in 1841.

---

6   Meacham, 2008

Jackson killed the bank so well that it took the money lenders a full century – until 1935 (with the passage of the National Bank Act of 1935) – to undo the damage and reach the same point in their schemes. Andrew Jackson once said, when asked what his greatest accomplishment as President was, that "I killed the Bank."

Black Friday, September 24, 1869

The following story by Robert J. McNamara[7] titled *The Black Friday Gold Corner* is an example of how easily the money supply can be manipulated when it consists of a precious metal, in this case gold. It is given in full because it reveals many interesting aspects of money supply manipulation.

"*Black Friday*, a financial crisis which came close to crashing the American economy, struck Wall Street on September 24, 1869. It was caused when the notorious speculators Jay Gould and Jim Fisk tried to corner the market on gold.

The audacious plan devised by Gould hinged on the fact that trading in gold had a great effect on the national economy in the years following the Civil War. And in the unregulated markets of the time, an unscrupulous character like Gould could conspire with other traders as well as government officials to subvert the market.

For Gould's plan to work, he and his partner Fisk needed to drive up the price of gold. Doing so would wipe out many traders and allow those in on the scheme to make outrageous profits.

A potential obstacle stood in way: the federal government. If the United States Treasury were to sell gold, flooding the

7   McNamara, 2017

market at the time Gould and Fisk were manipulating the market to cause the price to rise, the conspirators would be thwarted.

To ensure no intervention from the government, Gould had bribed government officials, including even the new brother in law of President Ulysses S. Grant. But despite his crafty planning, Gould's plan came apart when the government entered the gold market and drove the prices down.

In the mayhem that reached a pinnacle on the day that became notorious as "Black Friday," September 24, 1869, the "gold ring," as the newspapers called it, was broken. Yet Gould and Fisk still profited, making millions of dollars for their efforts.

Bribes Paved the Way for Gould's Scheme

Jay Gould, who would become known as a classic robber baron, had been working on Wall Street for ten years by the time he devised his plan to control the gold market.

And like many unscrupulous traders of his era, he was familiar with the technique of "cornering."

Cornering is a technique which has since been outlawed, but in the free-wheeling stock markets of the 1860s it was not uncommon. The mechanics of a stock market corner could become quite complicated, but in simple terms it meant that traders acting together could quietly buy up as much of the supply of a stock as they could. Once they controlled the stock, they could dictate the price.

When Gould first attempted a corner on the gold supply in the summer of 1869 he quickly learned that government intervention could quickly derail his plans. He needed to find a way to keep the federal government on the side-lines.

Gould had close connections to New York's Tammany Hall political machine, and he was experienced in bribing politicians. And he found a way into the Grant administration through Abel Corbin, an acquaintance who just married President Grant's sister.

Gould bribed Corbin to set up a meeting with Grant. Speaking with Grant in a social setting, Gould tried to influence the president's views on gold sales. Grant was not convinced of Gould's arguments, so Gould made sure to bribe officials.

After the scheme collapsed, it was widely assumed that Gould had bribed a war hero who had been appointed to an important treasury post in New York City, General Daniel Butterfield, who is best remembered for having composed the bugle call "Taps."

The Black Friday Panic

Gould, Fisk, and others in on the scheme began buying gold in earnest in September 1869, and as the month went on the price steadily rose. Finally, the gold market opened in a frenzy on the morning of Friday, September 24, 1869.

It appears that Jay Gould had hints that his plan to keep the federal government from intervening was doomed. And while the traders at the gold exchange in lower Manhattan furiously drove the price upward, he began selling the gold shares.

By midday the word came out that the federal government would sell gold supplies to lower the price. The scheme had been thwarted, and many traders were ruined. Gould, as he had sold off his positions before the price collapse happened, escaped with a huge profit that some estimates placed as high as $10 million.

Remarkably, much of the manipulation of the market

happened in plain view of the public. The New York Sun devoted most of its front page to stories about "the gold ring" on September 25, 1869. Details of the day's trading were meticulously reported, and an unethical scheme to rig one of the most important markets in the country was reported with the liveliness of a sporting event."

What is really astonishing in this story is that two individuals could have such a tremendous effect on a country's economy by manipulating the money supply.

The Deflation After the American Civil War

The following excerpt is taken from the documentary *The Money Masters* by Bill Still and Patrick S.J. Carmack[8].

"(After the Civil War) .... the Money Changers wanted two things: 1) the re-institution of a privately-owned central bank under their exclusive control, and, 2) an American currency issued by them and backed by their gold.

Their strategy was two-fold: first, to cause a series of panics to try to convince the American people that the existing decentralized banking system did not work and that only centralized control of the money supply could provide economic stability; and secondly, to remove so much money from the system that most Americans would be so desperately poor that they either wouldn't be patient enough to fight for true reform, or would be too weak to oppose the bankers, who would offer them relief if the bankers' plans were approved: in short, to convince Americans it was worth the long-term risk to freedom to obtain short-term economic relief.

In 1866, there was $1,800,000,000 in currency in circulation

---

8   Still and Carmack, 1996

in the United States - about $50.46 per capita. In 1867 alone, $500,000,000 was removed from the U.S. money supply. Ten years later, in 1876, America's money supply was reduced to only $600,000,000. In other words, two-thirds of America's money had been called in by the bankers. Incredibly, only $14.60 per capita remained in circulation.

Ten years later, the money supply had been further reduced to only $400,000,000, even though the population had boomed. The result was that only $6.67 per capita remained in circulation, an 84% decline in just 20 years. The people suffered terribly in a protracted, severe depression.

Today, bank-funded economists try to sell the idea that recessions and depressions are a natural part of something they call the "business cycle." One economist actually tried to explain business cycles with reference to sun spots! The truth is, our money supply is completely manipulated now, just as it was after the Civil War, just as it was by Nicholas Biddle and the 2nd BUS (Bank of the United States).

How did money become so scarce? Simple - bank loans were called in and no new ones were given. In addition, Greenbacks were retired by the millions and silver coins were melted down."

On January 17, 1873, a harmless looking Bill entitled *An Act Revising and Amending the Laws Relative to the Mints, Assay Offices and the Coinage of the United States* was passed by the Senate. It proved to be a camouflaged bill to demonetize silver so that the currency in the United States could be further contracted and the bankers gain more complete control of the monetary system.

General Grant, who signed the Bill as President, stated later that he had signed the document without reading it on the representation that it was merely a bill to reform coinage and mint laws, and had no intimation that it demonetized silver. Moreover, according to the Congressional Record, none but the members of the Committee that introduced the Bill understood its meaning.

According to a sworn affidavit dated May 9, 1892, given by Mr. Frederick A. Luckenbach, his friend Mr. Ernest Seyd - a supposed authority on the coining of money, and a representative of the Bank of England - was sent by the Governors of the Bank of England to America in the winter of 1872-73, with 100,000 pounds sterling in his pocket. He had the authority to draw on the Bank for as much more as was required to accomplish the Bank's objective. He was invited to sit with the Committee and to offer his assistance in the drafting of the Bill "To Reform Coinage and Mint Laws". He later said:

> "I saw the Committee of the House and Senate and paid the money and stayed in America until I knew the measure was safe."

This nefarious plot became known as the "Crime of 1873".

In 1872, silver had also been demonetized in France, Germany, England and Holland. Thus, there seems to be little doubt that this was part of a synchronized scheme coordinated by the international bankers in order to establish the gold standard in the world.

As mentioned earlier in this section, the gold standard created chaos on the American economy and enabled private bankers to withhold loans and restrict the money supply at will.

Germany's 1923 Hyperinflation

Stephen Zarlenga wrote in his book *Lost Science of Money*: [9]

"The great German hyperinflation of 1922-23 is one of the most widely cited examples by those who insist that private bankers, not governments, should control the money system. What is practically unknown about that sordid affair is that it occurred under the auspices of a privately owned and controlled central bank...

"On May 26, 1922, the law establishing the independence of the Reichsbank and withdrawing from the Chancellor of the Reich any influence on the conduct of the Bank's business was promulgated. This granting of total private control over the German currency became a key factor in the worst inflation of modern times."

It was Hjalmar Schacht, the famous German banker who inspired the MEFO bills described in Chapter 3, himself who revealed what really happened. He wrote in his book *The Magic of Money:* [10]

"Towards the end of November the Dollar reached an exchange rate of 12 million Marks on the free market of the Cologne bourse. This speculation was not only hostile to the country's economic interests, it was also stupid. In previous years such speculation had been carried on either with loans which the Reichsbank granted lavishly, or with emergency money which one printed oneself, and then exchanged for Reichsmarks.

Now, however, three things had happened. The emergency money had lost its value. It was no longer possible to exchange it for Reichsmarks. *The loans formerly easily obtainable from the*

---

9   Zarlenga, 2002, p. 579

10   Schacht, 1967, pp. 69-70

Reichsbank were no longer granted, [11] and the Rentenmark could not be used abroad. For amongst the stipulations governing the issue of the Rentenmark, there was one which forbade the surrender of Rentenmarks to foreigners. For these reasons the speculators were unable to pay for the Dollars they had bought when payment became due. They were forced to sell the Dollars back, and the Reichsbank was not prepared to pay more than the official rate of 4.2 billion Marks to the Dollar. The speculators made considerable losses."

As Zarlenga explains:

"Schacht is telling us that the excessive speculation against the Mark - the short selling of the mark - was financed by lavish loans from the private Reichsbank. The margin requirements that the anti-mark speculators needed and without which they could not have attacked the Mark was provided by the private Reichsbank."

The Great Depression

The Federal Reserve undertook a large purchase program in 1927, purchasing 300 million dollars of government securities and reducing the discount rate. This was supposedly done to increase the money supply and boost economic activity. However, hardly any of this money created out of thin air went into productive investments, but found its way into the stock market, where the cyclically adjusted price-to-earnings (CAPE) ratio moved above 30 for the first time in history.

In fact, according to Coogan (1963):

"In August of 1927, despite opposition from eleven of the twelve Federal Reserve Banks, who saw the danger, the

---

11   Ed: The italics are ours

Central Federal Reserve Banks were ordered to lower their re-discount rates and buy additional Government bonds. In other words, the steps were taken to increase the reserves of the city banks. City banks responded by increasing their promises-to-pay (loans). These loans went almost entirely to finance stock purchases. Loans were made on any and every kind of collateral. It became a very common practice for corporations to issue rights to buy additional stocks, and for individuals exercising those rights to borrow the entire amount at their banks, using the stock as collateral. In other words, banks were creating promises-to-pay and the funds thus created were flowing into the treasuries of corporations, there either to lie idle as deposit cash or to be used in building plants. Of course, these loans were unsound.

This was the actual method of financing the terrific stock market speculation of 1928-29; it was not "prosperity" as many supposed. The rural sections were being deliberately drained of their money by coercing country bankers into calling their local loans and purchasing very questionable domestic bonds and international loans. These orders came from the bank examiners acting under the authority of the United States Treasury which, of course, was dominated by the Federal Reserve policies. Honest country bankers protested that their communities needed whatever funds existed, but they were told to either comply with the examiners' orders or get out of the banking business. In response to the stimulation of bank loans (promises-to-pay) flowing into the stock market, the price of securities rose higher and higher. Stocks of corporations which had very little property and whose earnings were small, sold at from 20 to 50 times their earnings. Conditions grew more dangerous and spectacular each day.

Thinking people knew that someday the bankers would begin to curtail their privately created money, loaned at interest—and when they did, the securities markets would suffer a terrific crash. That crash would destroy billions of dollars' worth of then existing purchasing power; would cancel the credit money then in use, and wreck countless individuals and businesses.

The newspapers and well publicized paid "Economists" repeated deliberate falsehoods telling the people that America was in a "new era." We were assured eternally rising prices and all of the old measurements of stock values were out-of-date. The New York Stock Exchange was an Aladdin's lamp. The newspapers did everything possible to fan the flames and 16,000,000 people in the United States were active participants in the purchase and sale of securities."

On February 6, 1929, Mr. Montagu Norman, Governor of the Bank of England, came to Washington and had a conference with Andrew Mellon, Secretary of the Treasury. Immediately after that mysterious visit, the Federal Reserve Board abruptly changed its policy and pursued a high discount rate policy, abandoning the cheap money policy which it had inaugurated in 1927 after Mr. Norman's other visit.

On March 9, 1929, Paul Warburg, founder of the Federal Reserve Bank, issued a tip to all member banks and the Secretary of the Treasury that the crash was coming. Before it did, John D. Rockefeller, Bernard Baruch, Joseph P. Kennedy, and other money barons got out of the market. Early withdrawal from the market not only preserved the fortunes of these men, it also enabled them to return later and buy up whole companies at a bargain.

On October 24, 1929, the Federal Reserve Bank suddenly decided to bring this wave of speculation to an abrupt end by increasing the re-discount rate to 6 per cent. As Coogan (1963) wrote:

"On October 24, 1929, at 11:00 o'clock sharp hundreds of thousands of shares in hundreds of issues were offered for sale "at the market." It was a very strange thing that this could have been a mere accident. It was most unusual that thousands of people decided to sell at the same instant. It was also strange that they all decided to sell "at the market." Inexperienced stock traders do not put in "market" orders. That's a trick known only to the "wise boys" — the internationalists and their cohorts, the type of government adviser speculator who says "a speculator has to be right."

The market continued to crash day after day. The new era was over. The internationalists had squeezed the money accordion. It was they who had pumped the air into it and it was now their privilege to let it out. They had no responsibility whatever to inform Mr. and Mrs. American that they had decided to curtail the credit. After all, it was their privilege to contract the volume of promises-to-pay (loans) outstanding; to pull gold out of the country, and to collapse the whole "price" and money structure. Was it not they who had expanded it? It was "legally" their instrument; theirs was the exclusive franchise to play it for private pleasure and personal profit."

According to an article titled *"The 1929 Stock Market Crash"* by Harold Bierman: [12]

"The 1929 stock market crash is conventionally said to have occurred on Thursday the 24th and Tuesday the 29th of October. These two dates have been dubbed "Black Thursday" and "Black Tuesday," respectively. On September 3, 1929, the Dow Jones Industrial Average reached a record high of 381.2. At the end of the market day on Thursday, October 24, the market was at 299.5 — a 21 percent decline from the high. On this day the market fell 33 points — a drop of 9 percent — on trading that was approximately three times the normal daily volume for the first nine months of the year. By all accounts, there was a selling panic. By November

---

12   Bierman, 2008

13, 1929, the market had fallen to 199. By the time the crash was completed in 1932, following an unprecedentedly large economic depression, stocks had lost nearly 90 percent of their value."

In October 1929 the monetary base was 7.345 billion dollars and by October 1930 it was 6.817 billion dollars. That's a drop of over 7 per cent, one of the largest declines in the 20th century.

In 1933, 25 percent of all workers and 37 percent of all non-farm workers in the United States were completely out of work. Some people starved; many others lost their farms and homes. Homeless vagabonds sneaked aboard the freight trains that crossed the nation. Although the U.S. economy began to recover in the second quarter of 1933, the recovery largely stalled for most of 1934 and 1935. A more vigorous recovery commenced in late 1935 and continued into 1937, when a new depression occurred. The American economy had yet to fully recover from the Great Depression when the United States was drawn into World War II in December 1941. Because of this agonizingly slow recovery, the entire decade of the 1930s in the United States is often referred to as the Great Depression. This is to be compared to the situation in National Socialist Germany in the 1930s, in which a country without gold and foreign exchange reserves got out of a deep recession by creating its own debt free and interest free money. This process will be described in Chapter 6.

Regarding the New York Stock Exchange collapse, Congressman Louis T. McFadden, who served as chairman of the United States House Committee on Banking (1920-1931), stated:

"It was a carefully contrived occurrence... The international bankers sought to bring about a condition of despair so that they might emerge as the rulers of us all."

He died under suspicious circumstances[13] on October 1, 1936, while visiting New York City with his family, after he had persistently talked about the U.S. Federal Reserve Bank's "gigantic train of crime".

As stated in the Introduction to this book, in November 8, 2002, at the Conference to Honour Milton Friedman in the University of Chicago, the then Governor of the Federal Reserve Board, Ben S. Bernanke, said:

"Regarding the Great Depression. You're right, we did it. We're very sorry. But thanks to you, we won't do it again."

It is to be noticed that the Austrian school theory of the business cycle explains very well the facts that occurred during the Great Depression. An increase of the money supply with money created out of thin air sends wrong signals to the economic agents. These embark on a series of malinvestments (badly allocated investments) and create a stock market bubble. When the bubble pops, a depression takes place that wreaks havoc in the economy and the social structure of the nation.

The Man Who Broke the Bank of England

It seems that the kind of money supply manipulation described in Chapter 5 (Black Friday) continues nowadays, albeit by using legal means. As an example we can refer to billionaire George Soros, who is known as "The man who broke the Bank of England." Indeed, see, for example, the following excerpt taken from the article published on the web page of the newspaper *The Telegraph*[14], whose author is David Litterick.

"As early as spring 1992, Mr. Soros had decided that the

---

13   Cook, 2008

14   Litterick, 2002

pound would have to be devalued because it had been pushed into the ERM (Exchange Rate Mechanism) at too high a rate.

He knew that the Bundesbank favoured a devaluation of both sterling and the Italian lira and believed it would have to happen because of the disastrous impact that high British interest rates were having on asset prices.

Mr. Soros spent the next few months building up a position from which he would profit from that devaluation. He borrowed sterling heavily, reportedly to the tune of £6.5 billion, and converted that into a mixture of Deutschmarks and French francs.

On Black Wednesday, Mr. Soros's bet paid off. In the following days, he unwound his positions, paying back his original borrowings and ending with a profit of around £1 billion. As a parallel play, Mr. Soros bought as much as £350 million of British shares at the same time, gambling that equities often rise after a currency devalues.

He admitted that his actions had benefited no one but himself and, at the time, claimed that the only thing that could save Britain was a common single currency - a view he continues to hold."

The Financial Crisis of 2007

In Episode 7 of the documentary series *Hidden Secrets of Money* by Mike Maloney[15], the lawyer and best seller financial author Jim Rickards stated:

"1998 was a warning. It started in 1997. Capital outflow from

---

15   Maloney, 2016

emerging countries started in Thailand, there was blood in the streets, and in Jakarta and Seoul, made its way to Russia, Russia imploded, took down the hedge fund long-term capital management. Finally, the world built a firewall around Brazil and Brazil did not collapse although it would have been the next domino to fall. There was a clear-cut lesson. Capital markets came within hours of complete closure. We did bring it in for a soft landing, but the world has kind of forgotten that episode. We were literally hours away from shutting down global bond markets.

There are some lessons that should have been learned. 1) Banks should have been broken into smaller units. 2) Derivatives should have been banned.

There are things that should have been learned from that. Instead, we did the opposite. 1) We repealed the Glass-Steagall Act (1933), which allowed banks to be hedge-funds. 2) We repealed Swaps Regulation, which allowed banks to create swaps and derivatives. 3) We repealed the Net Capital Rule for Brokers/Dealers, so instead of 15 to 1 leverage, we allowed 30 to 1 leverage. 4) We implemented Basel II, which allowed banks to use more leverage. We did exactly the opposite of what we should have learned in 1998."

In view of the previous remarks, the Financial Crisis of 2007 did not come as a surprise.

According to an article titled *"What Caused the 2008 Global Financial Crisis?"* by Kimberly Amadeo: [16]

"The financial crisis was primarily caused by deregulation in the financial industry. That permitted banks to engage in hedge fund trading with derivatives. Banks then demanded more mortgages to support the profitable sale of these

---

16   Amadeo, 2017

derivatives. They created interest-only loans that became affordable to sub-prime borrowers.

In 2004, the Federal Reserve raised the fed funds rate just as the interest rates on these new mortgages reset.

Housing prices started falling as supply outpaced demand. That trapped home-owners who couldn't afford the payments, but couldn't sell their house. When the values of the derivatives crumbled, banks stopped lending to each other. That created the financial crisis that led to the Great Recession."

The events unfolded in the following way. Towards the end of President Clinton's Administration, there was a political campaign favouring the right of everyone to own a home. For this reason, the Department of Housing and Development initiated a program called National Home-ownership Strategy: Partners in the American Dream. As a result, credit standards and regulations were relaxed and low "teaser" interest rates were offered that ratcheted up significantly after two years. Loans were devised that required only the payment of interest, not principal, as well. Mortgages were extended to 50-year terms to reduce monthly payments.

Between 1997 and 2006, the price of the typical American house increased by 124 per cent, but in 2008 it experienced a drop of 20 per cent. During the two decades ending in 2001, the national median home price ranged from 2.9 to 3.1 times median household income. This ratio rose to 4.0 in 2004, and 4.6 in 2006.

Two products that caused the crisis were collateralized debt obligations and credit default swaps. A collateralized debt obligation (CDO) can be thought of as a promise to pay investors in a prescribed sequence, based on the cash flow the CDO collects from the pool of bonds or other assets it owns. CDOs packaged mortgages and other forms of debt into "bundles" for resale to gullible investors. Because CDOs included so many forms of bundled debt, assessing their risk was particularly tricky. However, rating agencies gave triple A ratings to CDOs on many occasions. A credit default swap (CDS) is a financial agreement according to which the seller of the CDS insures the buyer against some reference loan defaulting. CDSs existed since 1994, and increased in use in the early 2000s. By the end of 2007, the outstanding CDS amount was 62.2 trillion dollars, falling to 26.3 trillion dollars by mid-year 2010 and reportedly 25.5 trillion dollars in early 2012.

CDOs and CDSs were aggressively marketed by the shadow banking sector, a set of institutions that includes investment banks and hedge funds, which operated as banks without being banks, raising resources in the short term, operating with very high leverage and investing in long-term and illiquid assets. Unlike banks, however, these institutions were loosely regulated and supervised, they did not have reserves of capital, and they had no access to deposit insurance, to the re-discount operations or to the last resort credit lines of central banks.

The housing bubble finally popped and on September 15, 2008, Lehman Brothers filed for bankruptcy. The Emergency Economic Stabilization Act of 2008 was passed on October 3, authorizing the United States Secretary of the Treasury to spend up to 700 billion dollars to purchase distressed assets, especially mortgage-backed securities, and supply cash directly to banks. It was a component of the government's measures in 2008 to address the sub-prime mortgage crisis. However, as of July, 2015, the total commitment of the government was 16.8 trillion dollars with 4.6 trillion dollars already paid out.

Finally in this section, we will comment on the inability of macroeconomic models to predict a crisis like that of 2007. In fact, Olivier Blanchard, the IMF's Economic Counsellor and head of its Research Department, wrote in an article titled

"Where Danger Lurks" [17],

"How should we modify our benchmark models—the so-called dynamic stochastic general equilibrium (DSGE) models that we use, for example, at the IMF to think about alternative scenarios and to quantify the effects of policy decisions? The easy and uncontroversial part of the answer is that the DSGE models should be expanded to better recognize the role of the financial system—and this is happening. But should these models be able to describe how the economy behaves in the dark corners?

Let me offer a pragmatic answer. If macroeconomic policy and financial regulation are set in such a way as to maintain a healthy distance from dark corners, then our models that portray normal times may still be largely appropriate. Another class of economic models, aimed at measuring systemic risk, can be used to give warning signals that we are getting too close to dark corners, and that steps must be taken to reduce risk and increase distance. Trying to create a model that integrates normal times and systemic risks may be beyond the profession's conceptual and technical reach at this stage."

In other words, macroeconomic models that do not take into account the monetary system are as useless to forecast the future as trying to predict the movement of objects in the sky without considering the law of gravitation.

Media Control

We could present many articles and summaries that show how media control is performed by the power elite.

We think that the following excerpt, taken from the documentary

---

17   Blanchard, 2014

The Money Masters by Bill Still and Patrick S.J. Carmack [18], is a good example.

"By World War I, the Money Changers with their dominant wealth, had seized control of most of the nation's press.

In a 1912 Senate Privileges and Elections Committee hearing, a letter was introduced to the Committee written by Representative Joseph Sibley (PA), a Rockefeller agent in Congress, to John D. Archbold, a Standard Oil employee of Rockefeller's, which read in part:

> "An efficient literary bureau is needed, not for a day or a crisis but a permanent healthy control of the Associated Press and kindred avenues. It will cost money but will be cheapest in the end."

John Swinton, the former Chief of Staff of the *New York Times*, called by his peers "the Dean of his profession," was asked in 1953 to give a toast before the New York Press Club. He responded with the following statement:

> "There is no such thing as an independent press in America, if we except that of little country towns. You know this and I know it. Not a man among you dares to utter his honest opinion. Were you to utter it, you know beforehand that it would never appear in print.

> I am paid one hundred and fifty dollars a week so that I may keep my honest opinion out of the newspaper for which I write. You too are paid similar salaries for similar services. Were I to permit that a single edition of my newspaper contained an honest opinion, my occupation - like Othello's - would be gone in less than twenty-four hours.

---

18   Still and Carmack, 1996

The man who would be so foolish as to write his honest opinion would soon be on the streets in search of another job. It is the duty of a New York journalist to lie, to distort, to revile, to toady at the feet of Mammon, and to sell his country and his race for his daily bread, or what amounts to the same thing, his salary.

We are the tools and the vassals of the rich behind the scenes. We are marionettes. These men pull the strings and we dance. Our time, our talents, our lives, our capacities are all the property of these men - we are intellectual prostitutes." (As quoted by T. St. John Gaffney in *Breaking The Silence*, page 4.)

That was the U.S. press in 1953. It is the mass media of America today.

Press control, and later electronic media control (radio and TV), was seized in carefully planned steps, yielding the present situation in which all major mass media and the critically important major reporting services, which are the source of most news and upon which most news is based, are controlled by the Money Changers.

Representative Callaway discussed some of this press control in the Congressional Record, Vol. 54, Feb. 9, 1917, p. 2947:

"In March, 1915, the J. P. Morgan interests, the steel, shipbuilding, and powder interests, and their subsidiary organizations, got together 12 men high up in the newspaper world and employed them to select the most influential newspapers in the United States and sufficient number of them to control generally the policy of the daily press. They found it was only necessary to purchase the control of 25 of the greatest papers... An agreement was reached; the policy of the papers was bought, to be paid for by the month; an editor was furnished for each paper to properly supervise and edit information regarding the questions of preparedness, militarism, financial policies, and other things of national and international nature considered vital to the interests of the purchasers."

G. Edward Griffin quoting Ferdinand Lundberg adds this detail:

"So far as can be learned, the Rockefellers have given up their old policy of owning newspapers and magazines outright, relying now upon the publications of all camps to serve their best interests in return for the vast volume of petroleum and allied advertising under Rockefeller control.

After the J .P. Morgan bloc, the Rockefellers have the most advertising of any group to dispose of. And when advertising alone is not sufficient to insure the fealty of a newspaper, the Rockefeller companies have been known to make direct payments in return for a friendly editorial attitude."

A few years ago, three-quarters of the majority stockholders of ABC, CBS, NBC and CNN were banks, such as Chase Manhattan Corp., Citibank, JP Morgan Guaranty Trust and Bank of America; ten such corporations controlled 59 magazines (including *Time* and *Newsweek*) , 58 newspapers (including the *New York Times*, the *Washington Post*, the *Wall Street Journal*), and various motion picture companies, giving the major Wall Street banks virtually total ownership of the mass media, with few exceptions (such as the Disney Company's purchase of ABC).

Only 50 cities in America now have more than one daily paper, and they are all owned by the same group. Only about 25% of the nation's 1,500 daily papers are independently owned. This concentration has been rapidly accelerating in recent years and ownership is nearly monolithic now, reflecting the identical control described above.

Of course, much care is taken to fool the public with the appearance of competition by maintaining different corporate logos, anchorpersons and other trivia, projecting a sense of objectivity that belies the uniform underlying bank ownership and editorial control. This accounts for the total blackout on news coverage and investigative reporting of banker control of our country.

Nevertheless, throughout U.S. history, the battle over who gets the power to issue our money has raged. In fact it has changed hands back and forth eight times since 1694, in five transition periods which may aptly be described as "Bank Wars" (or more precisely: Private Central Bank vs. American People Wars), yet this fact has virtually vanished from public view for over three generations behind a smoke screen emitted by Fed cheerleaders in the media.

Until we stop talking about "deficits" and "government spending" and start talking about who creates and controls how much money we have, it's just a shell game - a complete and utter deception. It won't matter if we pass an iron-clad amendment to the Constitution mandating a balanced budget. Our situation is only going to get worse until we root out the cause at its source.

Our leaders and politicians need to understand, those few who are not part of the problem, what is happening, and how, as well as what solutions exist. The government must take back the power to issue our money, without debt.

Issuing our own debt-free money is not a radical solution. It's the same solution proposed at different points in U.S. history by men like Benjamin Franklin, Thomas Jefferson, Andrew Jackson, Martin Van Buren, Abraham Lincoln, William Jennings Bryan, Henry Ford, Thomas Edison, numerous Congressmen and economists.

So, to sum the economic problem up: in 1913, Congress delegated to a privately owned central bank, deceptively named the Federal Reserve System, control over the quantity of America's money, virtually all of which is created in parallel with an equivalent quantity of debt."

Income Inequalities

In our opinion, the following article by Charles Hugh-Smith entitled *If we Don't Change the way Money is Created and Distributed, we Change Nothing* exemplifies very well what is the situation today with respect to income inequalities and this is the reason why we present it in full. It is taken from the *"Zerohedge"* web page. [19]

"The only real solution in my view is to create and distribute money at the base of the pyramid rather than to those in the top of the pyramid.

Many well-intended people want to reform the status quo for all sorts of worthy reasons: to reduce wealth inequality, restore democracy, create good-paying jobs, and so on. All these goals are laudable, but if we don't change the way money is created and distributed, nothing really changes: wealth inequality will keep rising, governance will remain a bidding process of the wealthy, wages will continue stagnating, etc. If the money creation/distribution system isn't transformed, "reform" is nothing more than ineffectual policy tweaks that offer do-gooders the illusion of progress.

Mike Swanson of Wall Street Window and I discuss the future of currencies and CHS's (Charles Hugh-Smith) New Book *A Radically Beneficial World.*

---

19   Hugh-Smith, 2015

Few are willing to admit that the way we create and distribute money at the top of the wealth pyramid necessarily generates increasing wealth inequality because once we admit this, we realize 1) the money system itself is the source of inequality and 2) we have to change the money system if we want to stave off the inevitable rise of wealth inequality to the point that it generates social disorder.

In the current system, money is created by central and private banks at the top of the wealth/power pyramid, and distributed within the top of the wealth pyramid. The only possible output of this system is rising wealth inequality and debt-serfdom for three reasons:

1. Those with first access to nearly free money can outbid savers and serfs who must borrow at much higher rates of interest to snap up income-producing assets. In effect, borrowing unlimited sums at near-zero rates guarantees that those with this privilege have a built-in advantage in buying income-producing assets. The only possible output of this system is the rich get richer as they buy up all the most profitable and lowest-risk income-producing assets.

2. Those who can borrow virtually unlimited sums at less than 1% interest skim vast wealth by loaning the money out to everyone below the top of the pyramid at 4% (mortgages), 8% (other loans), and 18% (credit cards). This funnels much of the national income stream to those who can borrow cheap and lend the money at much higher rates.

3. Since the wealthy already own most of the income-producing assets, the easiest way to boost their wealth is to bid up those assets with cheaply borrowed money. For example, borrowing $100 million and using it for stock buybacks leverages the value of the shares by far more than $100 million.

Three different perspectives of the wealth pyramid illustrate how our money system generates wealth inequality as the only possible output of the system:

The system of central banks, private banks and fractional reserve lending is global. The net result is that globally, the vast majority of wealth is owned and controlled by those at the very apex of the wealth/power pyramid: the top 8% own 85% of global wealth.

In the U.S., the wealth-income pyramid can be represented by an inverted pyramid: the bulk of wealth and income are in the hands of the top 5%. The bottom 80% own an essentially trivial percentage of the national wealth.

This pyramid illustrates how the money creation and distribution pyramid works:

There are a number of proposed alternatives to this the rich can only get richer and the rest of us can only get poorer system. The only real solution in my view is create and distribute money at the base of the pyramid, to those generating useful goods and services in the community economy, rather than to those in the top of the pyramid. This money isn't borrowed into existence, so there is no interest to be skimmed by its creation."

Political Intervention

In this section, we will present several examples in history of political intervention on the part of the power elite.

The following excerpt is taken from the documentary *The Money Masters*[20].

---

20   Still and Carmack, 1996

"By cooperating within the family, using fractional reserve banking techniques, the Rothschilds' banks soon grew unbelievably wealthy. By the mid-1800s, they dominated all European banking, and were certainly the wealthiest family in the world. A large part of the profligate nobility of Europe became deeply indebted to them.

In virtue of their presence in five nations as bankers, they were effectively autonomous - an entity independent from the nations in which they operated. If one nation's policies were displeasing to them or their interests, they could simply do no further lending there, or lend to those nations or groups opposed to such policies. Only they knew where their gold and other reserves were located, thus shielding them from government seizure, penalty, pressure or taxation, as well as effectively making any national investigation or audit meaningless. Only they knew the extent (or paucity) of their fractional reserves, scattered in five nations - a tremendous advantage over purely national banks engaging in fractional reserve banking too.

It was precisely their international character that gave them unique advantages over national banks and governments, and that was precisely what rulers and national parliaments should have prohibited, but did not. This remains true of international or multi-national banks to this very day, and is the driving force of globalization - the push for one-world government.

The Rothschilds provided huge loans to establish monopolies in various industries, thereby guaranteeing the borrowers' ability to repay the loans by raising prices without fear of price competition, while increasing the Rothschild's economic and political power.

They financed Cecil Rhodes, making it possible for him to establish a monopoly over the gold fields of South Africa and the deBeers over diamonds. In America, they financed the monopolization of rail-roads.

The National City Bank of Cleveland, which was identified in Congressional hearings as one of three Rothschild banks in the United States, provided John D. Rockefeller with the money to begin his monopolization of the oil refinery business, resulting in Standard Oil.

Jacob Schiff, who had been born in the Rothschild "Green Shield" house in Frankfort and who was then the principal Rothschild agent in the U.S., advised Rockefeller and developed the infamous rebate deal Rockefeller secretly demanded from rail-roads shipping competitors' oil.

These same rail-roads were already monopolized by Rothschild control through agents and allies J. P. Morgan and Kuhn, Loeb & Company (Schiff was on the Board) which together controlled 95% of all U.S. rail-road mileage.

By 1850, James Rothschild, the heir of the French branch of the family, was said to be worth 600 million French francs - 150 million more than all the other bankers in France put together. James had been established in Paris in 1812 with a capital of $200,000 by Mayer Amschel. At the time of his death in 1868, 56 years later, his annual income was $40,000,000. No fortune in America at that time equalled even one year's income of James. Referring to James Rothschild, the poet Heinrich Heine said: "Money is the god of our times, and Rothschild is his prophet."

James built his fabulous mansion, called Femeres, 19 miles north-east of Paris. Wilhelm I, on first seeing it exclaimed, "Kings couldn't afford this. It could only belong to a Rothschild." Another 19th century French commentator put it this way;

"There is but one power in Europe and that is Rothschild."

There is no evidence that their predominant standing in European or world finance has changed, to the contrary, as their wealth has increased they have simply increased their "passion for anonymity." Their vast holdings rarely bear their name.

Author Frederic Morton wrote of them that they had "conquered the world more thoroughly, more cunningly, and much more lastingly than all the Caesars before…"

The following article by Larry Elliott, economics editor, titled *World's eight richest people have same wealth as poorest 50%* appeared in the British newspaper *The Guardian*[21].

"The world's eight richest billionaires control the same wealth between them as the poorest half of the globe's population, according to a charity warning of an ever-increasing and dangerous concentration of wealth.

In a report published to coincide with the start of the week-long World Economic Forum in Davos, Switzerland, Oxfam said it was "beyond grotesque" that a handful of rich men headed by the Microsoft founder Bill Gates are worth $426bn (£350bn), equivalent to the wealth of 3.6 billion people…"

The following excerpt has been taken from the article by Daisy Luther titled *What Does The Future Hold For 'Average Joes'?*[22] that appeared in the *"Zerohedge"* web page.

"Editor's Comment: It is difficult to say exactly how, or when, the next collapse will be triggered, but of course all the conditions are ripe for it.

---

21   Elliott, 2017

22   Luther, 2017

What can be certain is that the technocrats intent on controlling the future are already engineering the post-collapse society. Many of the Davos elite have been pushing "universal basic income" for all countries across the globe, and are leading people not only into a digital grid where cash is banned, but also into a society where private property and ownership are outlawed.

They are designing a future in which you must borrow or rent everything you need from corporations or the government, if you are allowed to have them at all..."

"You Realize The Universal Basic Income Is Feudalism, Right?

by Daisy Luther

What does the future hold for average people?

Feudalism.

And they'll welcome it with open arms, convinced that they are embracing a smart, fair system that eliminates poverty. The greed, entitlement, and lack of ambition that seems inherent in many people today will have them slipping on the yoke of servitude willingly..."

The author encourages readers to see the rest of the article because it is very enlightening as to the future that awaits us if we do not take action to remedy it. The first step in this direction would be the abolition of the present monetary system and its substitution with another one along the lines described in the last chapter of this book.

Academia Control

In this section, we present some examples of academics expressing false ideas about economics. The doubt persists whether these people lie deliberately or they are so biased by their education that they do not realize they are completely mistaken.

We begin with the banning of cash. Since central banks have no other choice than to continue imposing negative interest rates, the only logical option is to ban cash and force consumers to hold their money within the banking system. This is the real reason to ban cash. In the article by Thorstein Polleit titled *Cash Banned, Freedom Gone*[23] some of the negative consequences of banning cash are discussed. For example:

> "If the state bans cash, all transactions must be executed electronically. For the state to see who buys what when and who travels when where is then only a small step away. The citizen thus becomes completely transparent and his financial privacy is being lost. Even the prospect that a citizen can be spied upon at any time is an infringement on his right of freedom."

To this one can add that it would be very easy for the State to put somebody virtually "in jail" by simply not allowing him to buy anything. However, some economists suggest that the main reason to ban cash is that it is easier to fight against crime, money laundering, etc.

For example, in the book *The Curse of Cash* by Kenneth S. Rogoff[24], this author supports the idea that cash should be banned for the reasons just mentioned. In fact, the author writes:

> "Has the time come for advanced-country governments to start phasing out paper currency (cash), except perhaps for small denomination notes, coins, or both? A huge number of economic, financial, philosophical, and even moral issues are buried in this relatively simple question. In this book, I

---

23   Polleit, 2016
24   Rogoff, 2016

argue, that, on balance, the answer is "yes". First, making it more difficult to engage in recurrent, large, and anonymous payments would likely have a significant impact on the discouragement of tax evasion and crime; even a relatively modest impact could potentially justify getting rid of most paper currency. Second, as I have argued for some time, phasing out paper currency is the simplest and most elegant approach to clearing the path for central banks to invoke unfettered negative interest rates policies should they bump up against the "zero lower bound" on interest rates."

The Spanish economist Jesús Fernández-Villaverde on September 11, 2016, also shares this view[25]:

"Let Us Ban Cash

The time has come to ban cash. It is an old institution, almost barbaric, that has grave negative consequences for human welfare. Banning it is not only possible, it is simple. Of all economic policy measures that western countries can take nowadays, there is no other one with so high benefits.

The reasons to ban cash are clear. We can divide them into two kinds, which I will refer to, in a rather imprecise manner, as macro and micro. Let us begin with the macro reasons...

The micro reasons to ban cash are well known. Most of cash is used in illegal activities (drugs, firearms transactions, bribes, fiscal fraud) and, although there are alternative ways (such as to pay with gold or diamonds), they are more troublesome. Most of us, thanks to credit and debit cards and Internet payments, already use very little cash. And in Scandinavia, its use is minimum. 500 euro and 100 dollar bills are employed in things that we do not like in our society."

---

25   Villaverde, 2016

Our next topic will be the nature and generation of money. In this respect, the last mentioned Spanish author offers the following contribution about money[26].

"To think about the dollar as Treasury debt has many advantages. I will only mention some of them...

The fourth advantage is that it provides us with a simple explanation about the origin of most central banks. Since the establishment of the first ones, like the Bank of England, central banks have been given a monopoly (or quasi-monopoly) to issue currency that can be used to pay taxes because this generates an enormous public debt market. Many thinkers, including Alexander Hamilton as a clear exponent, have argued that such a market has its advantages. For example, public debt generates assets that can be used as collateral and without which many economic transactions are not possible or changes in the labour market profile are produced; indeed, there is a very convincing argument supporting the idea that one of the problems of the world economy is that right now there is too little public debt in circulation."

The New Yorker's John Cassidy asked the Nobel Prize co-winner in Economics in 2013, Eugene Fama, how he thought the efficient-market hypothesis had held up during the recent financial crisis. The new Nobel laureate responded:

"I think it did quite well in this episode. Prices started to decline in advance of when people recognized that it was a recession and then continued to decline. There was nothing unusual about that. That was exactly what you would expect if markets were efficient."

When Cassidy mentioned the credit bubble that led to the housing bubble and ultimate bust, the famed professor said:

---

26   Villaverde, 2015

"I don't even know what that means. People who get credit have to get it from somewhere. Does a credit bubble mean that people save too much during that period? I don't know what a credit bubble means. I don't even know what a bubble means. These words have become popular. I don't think they have any meaning."

The following is an excerpt from an interview made on August 12, 2011, by the journalist Fareed Zakaria to Nobel Prize winner Paul Krugman (2008) and Former IMF Chief Economist Ken Rogoff in which Krugman calls for space aliens to fix the U.S. Economy.

Ken Rogoff: Infrastructure spending, if it were well-spent, that's great. I'm all for that. I'd borrow for that, assuming we're not paying Boston Big Dig kind of prices for the infrastructure.

Fareed Zakaria: But even if you were, wouldn't John Maynard Keynes say that if you could employ people to dig a ditch and then fill it up again, that's fine, they're being productively employed, they'll pay taxes, so maybe Boston's Big Dig was just fine after all.

Paul Krugman: Think about World War II, right? That was actually negative social product spending, and yet it brought us out. I mean, probably because you want to put these things together, if we say, "Look, we could use some inflation." Ken and I are both saying that, which is, of course, anathema to a lot of people in Washington but is, in fact, what basic logic says.

It's very hard to get inflation in a depressed economy. But if you had a program of government spending plus an expansionary policy by the Fed, you could get that. So, if you think about using all of these things together, you could accomplish a great deal. If we discovered that space aliens were planning to attack and we needed a massive build-up to counter the space alien threat and really inflation and budget deficits took secondary place to that, this slump would be over in 18 months. And then if we discovered, oops, we made a mistake, there aren't any aliens, we'd be better.

Ken Rogoff: And we need Orson Welles, is what you're saying.

Paul Krugman: No, there was a Twilight Zone episode like this in which scientists fake an alien threat in order to achieve world peace. Well, this time... we need it in order to get some fiscal stimulus.

Finally, we make the observation that no one of the leading economists or Nobel Prize laureates in Economics in the last forty years have signalled our monetary system as the prime cause of the depressions and rampant inequalities that we have been experiencing over that period of time and that have the cause in the perverse monetary system that was inaugurated with the creation of the Bank of England three hundred years ago. This is an indication that the Academia is under total control of the power elite nowadays and that this control has accentuated in the last forty years.

Critique of the Austrian School Proposal for the Money Supply

The Austrian School of Economics proposes that the money supply be completely backed by some commodity, usually gold, while issued and controlled by a private elite. As we have seen before in this chapter, this elite could cause depressions and inflations at will, looking always for their profit. Thus, the general public would not see the benefits of this monetary reform. Only the members of the elite controlling the money supply would benefit from it.

Huerta de Soto, the most prominent and prestigious Spanish economist belonging to the Austrian School, even proposes what he calls anarcho-capitalism[27]. This would imply the abolition of the state and the complete control of the economy by private individuals.

According to Von Mises in his book *Theory of Money and Credit*[28], "The concept of money as creature of law and the State is clearly untenable. It is not justified by a single phenomenon of the market." But he gives no explanation of this weird statement. We have documented case histories in this book that prove him wrong.

However, as mentioned in the Introduction to this book, the Austrian School condemns clearly and unequivocally the practice of fractional reserve banking.

---

27   de Soto, 2009

28   von Mises, 1934, p. 69

Chapter VI

Money Supply in Public Hands

In this chapter, we will present some examples in history in which the money supply was issued and controlled by the state. The same pattern arises in general. When the money supply is in public hands, people are usually happy, there is peace and prosperity, there are few inequalities, and there is no inflation. However, if the money supply is issued and controlled by a private elite, we have all the problems that we described in the previous chapter.

Money in Rome Under Julius Caesar

Julius Caesar (c. July 12 or 13, 100 BC to March 15, 44 BC) was born into a patrician family and is considered to be one of the greatest military commanders in history. The military campaigns of Julius Caesar constituted both the Gallic War (58 BC-51 BC) and Caesar's civil war (50 BC-45 BC). He decisively defeated Pompey, despite Pompey's numerical advantage (nearly twice the number of infantry and considerably more cavalry), at Pharsalus in an exceedingly short engagement in 48 BC. After that, he became the uncontested leader of Rome.

A monetary crisis followed the Civil War period due to a shortage of cash. An enormous quantity of coin had been taken to pay the rival armies in the conflict, and hoarding had withheld vast sums of cash from general circulation and banks. Consequently, money had become so scarce that there was simply not enough cash available to repay the outstanding levels of debt.

When Caesar returned to Italy in 45 BC, he found many

homeless people in the cities who had been expelled from the land by money lenders and landowners. There were three hundred and twenty thousand persons at Rome to whom grain was distributed.

Many of the leading Senators were in fact money lenders themselves who sought governorships through which they could become wealthy. They were charging interest rates as high as 48 per cent per annum.

According to T.E. Watson[1], and referring to Caesar:

> "He recognized the profound truth that money is a national agent, created by law for a national purpose, and that no classes of men should withhold it from circulation so as to cause panics, in order that speculators could advance the rates of interest, or could buy up property at ruinous prices after such panic."

To remedy this situation, Caesar made some social and monetary reforms. Among the latter, we can mention the following.

- He took back from the money lenders the power to coin money.

- He minted gold coins, at 1/40th of the Roman pound (about 8 g.). The main Roman denominations were linked following the equation, 1 aureus = 25 denarii = 100 sestertii = 400 asses. The Roman monetary system was stabilized for three centuries, and inflation was eradicated.

- He demanded that creditors not merely be obliged to accept real estate and movable objects in repayment, he also decreed that the valuations on such property would be established at pre-crash levels.

---

1   Watson, 2011, pp. 84-85

- He decreed that all interest previously paid by debtors to their creditors should be deducted from the principle of the loan in question.

- He established the annual rate of interest at no higher than 12 per cent.

With this new plentiful supply of money, Caesar built great public works projects and won the love of the common people. However, the previous measures caused great concern in Rome's power elite. Four years after assuming power, on March 15, 44 BC, he was assassinated.

Medieval England and the Tally Sticks

During the reign of King Edward I (1272-1307) of England, Statutes of the Jewry were passed in 1233 and 1275 which abolished all forms of usury. Since it was discovered that many Jews widely but secretly continued to practice usury, an edict called the Edict of Expulsion was issued by the same king on July 18, 1290, expelling the entire Jewish population from England. The Edict remained in effect for the rest of the Middle Ages, and it was over 350 years until it was formally overturned under Oliver Cromwell in 1657.

After the abolition of usury and the expulsion of the money lenders, taxes were tolerable and there was no state debt and no inflation. This was due to the existence of a sufficient quantity of money supply, an important part of which consisted of the tally sticks that we described in Chapter 3 and which were shown to be sound fiat money. The rest were metal coins issued by the King. The money supply was completely controlled by the state and the money was issued interest free and without debt.

With this system, a contented and prosperous life was enjoyed by all the inhabitants of England. In fact, according to R.K. Hoskins in his book *War Cycles - Peace Cycles*[2], Lord Leverhulme, a writer on that period, stated "The men of the 15th century were very well paid."

This golden era came to an end in the 17th century, when usury, as defined in this book, was introduced again, first in Holland and then in England.

President Lincoln and the Greenbacks

We have seen in Chapter 6 that President Lincoln's government was able to bypass the money lenders by issuing its own money, the Greenbacks, without interest and without debt. Due to Lincoln's assassination, which seems to have been perpetrated by an agent of the international bankers[3], the United States did not continue with this form of money issuance. However, to see what panic this experiment had caused among the central bankers, it is interesting to see what the London *Times* wrote in response to Lincoln's Greenback notes.

> "If this mischievous financial policy, which has its origin in North America, shall become endurated down to a fixture, then that Government will furnish its own money without cost. It will pay off debts and be without debt. It will have all the money necessary to carry on its commerce. It will become prosperous without precedent in the history of the world. The brains, and wealth of all countries will go to North America. That country must be destroyed or it will destroy every monarchy on the globe."

---

2   Hoskins, 1985, p. 54

3   Still and Carmack, 1996

Money Under Napoleon

Napoleon Bonaparte, after assuming power as First Consul on November 9, 1799, created the Banque de France as a joint stock company to foster economic recovery after the strong recession of the revolutionary period. To avoid monetary disorders, this new institution, that started operations on February 20, 1800, received the monopoly to issue banknotes in the Paris area.

Napoleon never issued fiat money inconvertible into gold and silver because he knew too well what happened to the Assignats, the paper money issued by the National Assembly in France from 1789 to 1796, during the French Revolution. He never debased the so called "franc germinal", established in 1803. One franc germinal was equivalent to 5 grams of silver and to 322 milligrams of gold. In fact, Napoleon built a monetary regime based on a bi-metal system (a combined gold and silver standard) that prevailed throughout the 19th century and made the franc the most stable currency in Europe.

The Bank listed among its founding shareholders Napoleon, members of his family, and several leading personalities of the time. The two hundred largest shareholders elected a board of 15 executives, who sat on the General Council administering the Bank, and three inspectors, who supervised the management of the Bank. The General Council in turn appointed a Central Committee consisting of a chairman and two more members.

Napoleon made himself president of the Bank. According to *Encyclopedia Britannica*, 1964, Vol. 3, p.132, he declared that:

> "The Bank does not belong to the shareholders only; it also belongs to the state, since the state has entrusted to it the privilege of issuing money. I wish the bank to be in sufficient measure in the hands of the state, but not too much so."

By means of two Acts of parliament, one on April 14, 1803,

and the other on April 22, 1806, Napoleon abolished the right of two rival banks to issue bank notes and replaced the three-member Central committee with a Governor and two Deputy Governors, respectively. The last Act also increased the Bank's capital to 90 million francs.

With these measures, Napoleon had no need for the loan markets of the city of London. This was probably the reason why England declared war on France in May 1803 when Napoleon refused to sign a trade treaty, thus starting the long period known as the Napoleonic wars.

The money supply in the Napoleonic period was not inflationary because the bank notes were all backed by gold and silver and fractional reserve banking was not allowed. In fact, he issued three decrees in 1808. The last one, to which the money lenders referred to as the *"Infamous Decree"*, severely restricted the practice of lending, and annulled all debts owed by married women, minors, and soldiers. Any loan that had an interest rate exceeding 10 percent was also annulled. A final decree was issued on July 20, 1808 ordering all Jews to adopt Surnames and to use those names on all documents.

On December 20, 1803, Napoleon obtained the money he needed for the war with a European Coalition set up by England against him by selling Louisiana to the United States for three million pounds in gold.

Money in the Russian Empire

In early 1815, during the Congress of Vienna, Nathan Mayer Rothschild approached Czar Alexander I (1801-1825) and proposed setting up a central bank in Russia, that could be controlled like other central banks such as the Bank of England. However, the Czar prudently declined.

As a consequence of this, it does not seem to be a coincidence that the last five Czars were assassinated, with an average age at death of 53, or that a Wall Street banker, Jacob Schiff, financed Leon Trotsky to overthrow the Russian monarchy[4].

The State Bank of the Russian Empire received its charter on 1 May 1860, and began operations in 1861 backed by a foreign loan. It was established originally as a commercial bank, designed to strengthen the Empire's payments system through the discounting of bills of exchange, the buying and selling of gold, silver and state bonds, to accept deposits and give out loans.

In the early 1880s the State Bank began to prepare a monetary reform, which was launched in 1895 and ended in 1898 with the introduction of gold monometallism in Russia. This reform also granted the State Bank the right to issue notes, but had to maintain 50 per cent gold backing up to a limit, and 100 per cent thereafter. It also minted the nation's coins and regulated the money supply. From 1894 the State Bank became the provider of credit to the commercial banks, through which low interest loans were provided to industry and commerce.

By 1914 it had become one of the most influential lending institutions in Europe, with gold reserves averaging over 100 per cent of deposits, while also acting as a major lender to industry and trade. By avoiding fractional reserve banking and by backing all notes and coins in circulation by gold, the State Bank provided the Russian economy with sound commodity and fiat money to carry out business in a noninflationary environment and with the smallest national debt in the world. During the last twenty years of peaceful imperial time (1895-1914) the increase in Gross Domestic Product averaged 10 per cent per annum and there was no unemployment. Elementary education was obligatory, and in 1912 Russia had the lowest levels of taxation in the world.

---

4   Sutton, 1981, p. 228

Three Monetary Experiments in the 1930s

In the 1930s, in the aftermath of the Great Depression, there were three countries that abandoned central banking and developed a new system in which the State would issue its own money, interest free and without debt, and commercial banks would not be allowed to practice fractional reserve banking. These countries were Germany, Italy and Japan. They would eventually sign in 1940 an alliance called "The Tripartite Pact". The economies of these countries were so successful in the 1930s, when other countries were in a severe depression, that many people think that war was waged on them to prevent other countries from following their example by issuing their own money, debt and interest free, through new state banks.

Money in National Socialist Germany

We have already described the case of Germany to a certain extent in Chapter 3. As mentioned there, the new money was introduced through the MEFO bills, which were discountable at the Reichsbank at a uniform rate of four per cent. They were drawn on three month's credit, but could be extended at three monthly intervals to a maximum of five years.

The system worked very well. After two years, unemployment had almost disappeared, and in five years Germany was the greatest economic power in the European continent. In the period 1933-1939, Germany had increased its Gross National Product by 100 per cent. In fact, according to Silverman, (1988):

"The recovery under Hitler, by 1935, from the low point in 1932 was as spectacular as the collapse (the depression from 1929 to 1932). Industrial production had rebounded by 66 per cent by 1935. Net national product at factor cost was up by 71 per cent. Weekly hours worked had risen by 7 per cent, the number of employed had climbed by 46 per cent, and average unemployment in 1935 was 61 per cent lower than in 1932. Only real hourly earnings failed to rise sharply; the 1935 level was less than 1 per cent higher than the 1932 level."

As regards trade, Germany had to resort to barter often in the period 1933-1937 to bypass the international payments system. According to Overy (1982):

"Imports were to be substituted by domestic production, and the only trade allowed was in essential raw materials and foodstuffs that could not be produced at home. Much of this trade was carried on through bilateral barter agreements through which special clearing arrangements could be made to avoid pressure on the balance of payments and Germany's very small stock of gold and foreign exchange."

Exports increased from RM4.9 billion in 1933 to RM5.9 billion in 1937 and RM5.3 billion in 1938, and the figures for imports were RM4.2 billion in 1933, RM5.5 billion in 1937 and RM5.4 in 1938.

As regards car production: [5]

"The years 1932-7 were the years when the motorization of Germany caught up with the levels achieved in other countries considerably earlier. A combination of government encouragement through propaganda and fiscal policy, increased agricultural prosperity (which encouraged farmers to buy vehicles) and a growing propensity among middle-class Germans to spend some of their growing savings on motor-cars, accounted for the buoyant growth of this particular sector."

In January 1939, the President of the Reichsbank, Hjalmar Schacht, refused to continue extending MEFO bills for fear of

---

5   Overy, 1982

inflation and sent Hitler a memorandum in which he expressed his viewpoint. Two weeks later Schacht was fired and a new Reichsbank law was passed on June 15, 1939, that made the bank "unconditionally subordinated to the sovereignty of the state." [6]

The MEFO bills were noninflationary because they were sound fiat money. That is, they were issued only against deliveries of good and services and were, therefore, backed by human labour.

Money in Italy Under Mussolini

In 1926 Mussolini had acquired full dictatorial powers and a new banking law was passed that, among other provisions, granted the Bank of Italy the exclusive right to issue banknotes and some supervisory powers. The establishment and merger of banks was to be authorized; a minimum capital according to the type of bank and area of operation was required, together with ratios of capital and reserves to deposits; and a limit to risk concentration was set.

As a consequence of the Wall Street crash of 1929, a disruptive crisis hit Italy in 1930-1931. In order to save the financial system, the government established in 1931 the *Istituto Mobiliare Italiano* to control and manage credit. Later on, the Institute for Industrial Reconstruction (IRI) acquired all shares previously held by banks in industrial, agricultural, and real estate enterprises. Italy abandoned the gold standard in 1934 and, with the passage of the Bank Reform Act in 1936, the Bank of Italy and most of the other major banks became government entities.

One can see the development of real GDP during the periods 1925-1936 and 2003-2014 in the graph [7] on the next page. The large jump in 1936 was the year in which the lira was sharply

---

6   Marsh, 1992

7   https://marketmonetarist.com/2014/11/15/italys-greater-depression-eerie-memories-of-the-1930s/

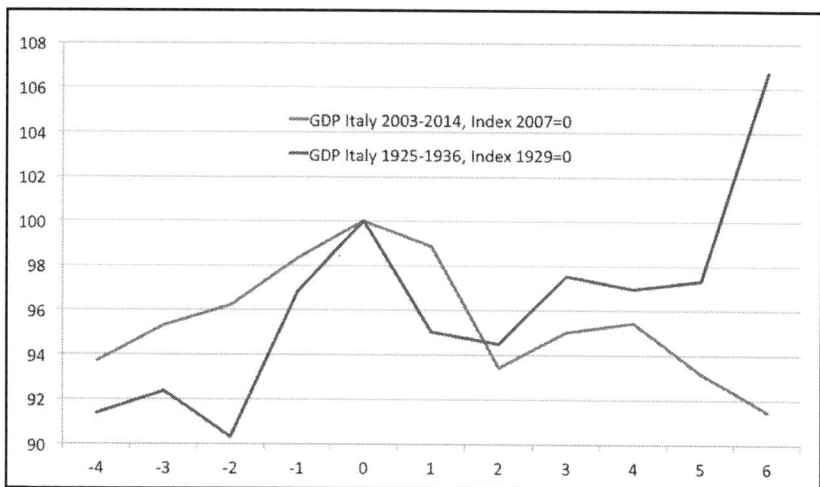

devalued. On the same page, the following comment is made. "By many measures, the Italian economy of today is worse than the Italian economy of the 1930s." It was the intervention of the state in the economy, mostly through the banking sector, which made the depression in Italy in the 1930s not as difficult as in other industrialized countries.

Money in Japan in the 1930's

Prior to the Meiji Restoration, Japan's feudal fiefs all issued their own money, hansatsu, but the *New Currency Act* of 1871 did away with these and established the *yen* as the new decimal currency. The former fiefs became prefectures and their mints became private chartered banks, which were initially allowed to retain the right to print money. For a time, both the central government and these so-called "national" banks issued money.

The Bank of Japan was founded on October 10, 1882, under the *Bank of Japan Act* of 1882 (June 27, 1882), after a Belgian model. It functioned as a typical central bank, i.e. for the benefit of a private elite, in spite of the fact that the Japanese Imperial Household was the largest shareholder. The institution was given a monopoly on controlling the money supply in 1884, but it would be another 20 years before the previously issued notes were retired.

On December 13, 1931, veteran Korekiyo Takahashi came back as Finance Minister for the fifth time in his career. Takahashi ordered a gold embargo on the day of his return to office. He went on to implement a series of economic policy adjustments over the next four years, until February 1936, when he was assassinated. His policy regime has since been referred to as the "Takahashi economic policy." This was a three-pronged macroeconomic policy with exchange rate, monetary, and fiscal dimensions.

On June 3, 1932, the government submitted a bill to issue deficit-covering bonds, together with a supplemental budget outlying expenditures for military action in Manchuria and for an emergency relief program in rural areas. Then, on the same day, Takahashi officially announced the Bank of Japan (BOJ) underwriting of government bonds. At the same time, the BOJ conducted an accommodative monetary policy by cutting its official discount rate in March, June, and August 1932. Meanwhile, the regulation on bank note issuance was amended in June to raise the limit of fiduciary note issuance from 120 million yen to 1 billion yen. From 1932 to 1936, the economy recovered under the "Takahashi Economic Policy" (Takahashi Zaisei), achieving a growth of 6.1 per cent in real Gross National Product (GNP) and an inflation, as measured by the GNP deflator, of 1.5 per cent. Unemployment was reduced from 6.88 per cent in 1932 to 2.27 per cent in 1939.

It was the previously described injection of sound fiat money into the economy through the state BOJ that saved Japan from the depression that affected most industrialized countries in the 1930s. The money was used in social and military spending. This was a noninflationary procedure because the money was not created by commercial banks through fractional reserve banking as is usually the case with central banking, but directly by the State.

The Bank of Japan Act of 1882 was replaced by the Bank of Japan Act of 1942, modelled after the German Reichsbank Law of 1939. The new act defined the BOJ as a state entity and strengthened the government's control on the BOJ's operations. It stipulated that the BOJ was to be responsible for the control of money, adjustment of finance, and reinforcement of the credit system in accordance with national policy, thereby fully utilizing the national economic power (Article 1). It was to devote itself entirely to achieving the national goal (Article 2). The BOJ was to issue banknotes for the benefit of all public and private transactions without any limit (Article 29).

Modern Examples of State-Issued Money

In this section, we will describe three examples of state-issued money. By this we mean states or communities that issue their own money interest free and without debt, and whose aim is the benefit of the state or the community and not that of a private elite.

Money in Gaddafi's Libya

Libya is a country in the Maghreb region of North Africa, bordered by the Mediterranean Sea to the north, Egypt to the east, Sudan to the south-east, Chad and Niger to the south and Algeria and Tunisia to the west.

On December 24, 1951, Libya declared its independence as the United Kingdom of Libya, a constitutional and hereditary monarchy under King Idris, Libya's only monarch. On September 1, 1969, a group of rebel military officers led by Muammar Gaddafi launched a coup d'état against King Idris and Gaddafi became the ruler of Libya.

In this section, we think that the article by Ellen Brown titled

"Libya: all About oil, or all About Banking?" [8] is very illustrative of the situation in Gaddafi's Libya and the events that led to Gaddafi's overthrow and death. It raises a lot of interesting points, including control of the nation's money. For this reason, we present the following excerpts.

"Several writers have noted the odd fact that the Libyan rebels took time out from their rebellion in March to create their own central bank – this before they even had a government. Robert Wenzel wrote in the Economic Policy Journal:

I have never before heard of a central bank being created in just a matter of weeks out of a popular uprising. This suggests we have a bit more than a rag tag bunch of rebels running around and that there are some pretty sophisticated influences.

Alex Newman wrote in the New American:

In a statement released last week, the rebels reported on the results of a meeting held on March 19. Among other things, the supposed rag-tag revolutionaries announced the "[d]esignation of the Central Bank of Benghazi as a monetary authority competent in monetary policies in Libya and appointment of a Governor to the Central Bank of Libya, with a temporary headquarters in Benghazi."

Newman quoted CNBC senior editor John Carney, who asked, "Is this the first time a revolutionary group has created a central bank while it is still in the midst of fighting the entrenched political power? It certainly seems to indicate how extraordinarily powerful central bankers have become in our era."

... Whatever might be said of Gaddafi's personal crimes, the Libyan people seem to be thriving. A delegation of medical professionals from Russia, Ukraine and Belarus wrote in an

---

8   Brown, 2011

appeal to Russian President Medvedev and Prime Minister Putin that after becoming acquainted with Libyan life, it was their view that in few nations did people live in such comfort:

[Libyans] are entitled to free treatment, and their hospitals provide the best in the world of medical equipment. Education in Libya is free, capable young people have the opportunity to study abroad at government expense. When marrying, young couples receive 60,000 Libyan dinars (about 50,000 U.S. dollars) of financial assistance. Non-interest state loans, and as practice shows, undated. Due to government subsidies the price of cars is much lower than in Europe, and they are affordable for every family. Gasoline and bread cost a penny, no taxes for those who are engaged in agriculture. The Libyan people are quiet and peaceful, are not inclined to drink, and are very religious.

They maintained that the international community had been misinformed about the struggle against the regime. "Tell us," they said, "who would not like such a regime?"

... Another explanation for the assault on Libya is that it is "all about oil," but that theory too is problematic. As noted in the National Journal, the country produces only about 2 percent of the world's oil. Saudi Arabia alone has enough spare capacity to make up for any lost production if Libyan oil were to disappear from the market. And if it's all about oil, why the rush to set up a new central bank?

Another provocative bit of data circulating on the Net is a 2007 "Democracy Now" interview of U.S. General Wesley Clark (Ret.). In it he says that about 10 days after September 11, 2001, he was told by a general that the decision had been made to go to war with Iraq. Clark was surprised and asked why. "I don't know!" was the response. "I guess they don't know what else to do!" Later, the same general said they planned to take out seven countries in five years: Iraq, Syria, Lebanon, Libya, Somalia, Sudan, and Iran.

What do these seven countries have in common? In the context of banking, one that sticks out is that none of them is listed among the 56 member banks of the Bank for International Settlements (BIS). That evidently puts them outside the long regulatory arm of the central bankers' central bank in Switzerland.

The most renegade of the lot could be Libya and Iraq, the two that have actually been attacked. Kenneth Schortgen Jr., writing on Examiner.com, noted that "[s]ix months before the US moved into Iraq to take down Saddam Hussein, the oil nation had made the move to accept Euros instead of dollars for oil, and this became a threat to the global dominance of the dollar as the reserve currency, and its dominion as the petrodollar."

According to a Russian article titled "Bombing of Libya – Punishment for Gaddafi for His Attempt to Refuse US Dollar," Gadaffi made a similarly bold move: he initiated a movement to refuse the dollar and the Euro, and called on Arab and African nations to use a new currency instead, the gold dinar. Gadaffi suggested establishing a united African continent, with its 200 million people using this single currency. During the past year, the idea was approved by many Arab countries and most African countries. The only opponents were the Republic of South Africa and the head of the League of Arab States. The initiative was viewed negatively by the USA and the European Union, with French president Nicolas Sarkozy calling Libya a threat to the financial security of mankind; but Gaddafi was not swayed and continued his push for the creation of a united Africa.

And that brings us back to the puzzle of the Libyan central bank. In an article posted on the Market Oracle, Eric Encina observed:

One seldom mentioned fact by western politicians and media pundits: the Central Bank of Libya is 100 per cent State owned.

. . Currently, the Libyan government creates its own money, the Libyan Dinar, through the facilities of its own central bank. Few can argue that Libya is a sovereign nation with its own great resources, able to sustain its own economic destiny. One major problem for globalist banking cartels is that in order to do business with Libya, they must go through the Libyan Central Bank and its national currency, a place where they have absolutely zero dominion or power-broking ability. Hence, taking down the Central Bank of Libya (CBL) may not appear in the speeches of Obama, Cameron and Sarkozy but this is certainly at the top of the globalist agenda for absorbing Libya into its hive of compliant nations.

Libya not only has oil. According to the IMF, its central bank has nearly 144 tons of gold in its vaults. With that sort of asset base, who needs the BIS, the IMF and their rules?

All of which prompts a closer look at the BIS rules and their effect on local economies. An article on the BIS website states that central banks in the Central Bank Governance Network are supposed to have as their single or primary objective "to preserve price stability." They are to be kept independent from government to make sure that political considerations don't interfere with this mandate. "Price stability" means maintaining a stable money supply, even if that means burdening the people with heavy foreign debts. Central banks are discouraged from increasing the money supply by printing money and using it for the benefit of the state, either directly or as loans.

In a 2002 article in Asia Times titled "The BIS vs National Banks," Henry Liu maintained:

BIS regulations serve only the single purpose of strengthening the international private banking system, even at the peril of national economies. The BIS does to national banking systems what the IMF has done to national monetary regimes. National economies under financial globalization no longer serve national interests.

. . . FDI [foreign direct investment] denominated in foreign currencies, mostly dollars, has condemned many national economies into unbalanced development toward export, merely to make dollar-denominated interest payments to FDI, with little net benefit to the domestic economies.

He added, "Applying the State Theory of Money, any government can fund with its own currency all its domestic developmental needs to maintain full employment without inflation." The "state theory of money" refers to money created by governments rather than private banks.

The presumption of the rule against borrowing from the government's own central bank is that this will be inflationary, while borrowing existing money from foreign banks or the IMF will not. But all banks actually create the money they lend on their books, whether publicly-owned or privately-owned. Most new money today comes from bank loans. Borrowing it from the government's own central bank has the advantage that the loan is effectively interest-free. Eliminating interest has been shown to reduce the cost of public projects by an average of 50 per cent.

And that appears to be how the Libyan system works. According to Wikipedia, the functions of the Central Bank of Libya include "issuing and regulating banknotes and coins in Libya" and "managing and issuing all state loans." Libya's wholly state-owned bank can and does issue the national currency and lend it for state purposes.

That would explain where Libya gets the money to provide free education and medical care, and to issue each young couple $50,000 in interest-free state loans. It would also explain where the country found the $33 billion to build the Great Man-Made River project. Libyans are worried that NATO-led air strikes are coming perilously close to this pipeline, threatening another humanitarian disaster.

... If the Gaddafi government goes down, it will be interesting to watch whether the new central bank joins the BIS, whether the nationalized oil industry gets sold off to investors, and whether education and health care continue to be free."

Money in the States of Guernsey

The island of Guernsey is located in the English Channel off the coast of Normandy. The jurisdiction embraces not only all ten parishes on the island of Guernsey, but also the much smaller inhabited islands of Herm, Jethou and Lihou together with many small islets and rocks. The jurisdiction is not part of the Commonwealth of Nations. However, defence and most foreign relations are handled by the British Government.

The following excerpts of the article *"Beating the Bankers at their Own Game – the Guernsey Way"* [9], published on April 22, 2016, describes the monetary experiment of Guernsey.

> "By the time Napoleon was finally defeated at Waterloo in 1815 life for people in Britain and especially Guernsey was hard. The effects of the Napoleonic wars had resulted in a state of despair on the part of the island community due to the acute economic distress then prevailing. Those that could were leaving the island and making their way to the mainland.
>
> ... A committee was appointed in 1815 to consider in particular the overcrowded state of the market.
>
> ... The committee examined the situation, and came to some rather sage conclusions:
>
> 1. Further taxation was impossible for the population to bear.

---

9   http://guernseydonkey.com/?p=12090

2. Borrowing money from the banks would entail the payment of a high rates of interest, which they could not afford, particularly in view of the fact that these interest payments would continue for years.

3. The States, if they were bold enough, could take advantage of their ancient prerogative and produce their own notes to finance the re-building of the market. (The rights and privileges to govern themselves since 1204 and guaranteed by successive Royal Charters)

They chose to go for option 3 and beat the bankers at their own game!

However, at first, this proposal to use issued currency to build a new market building was turned down. But later in that same year a different opportunity came along for which this proposal to issue State notes was agreed. The finance committee reported that £5,000 was needed for roads and a monument to the late Governor, but they had only £1,000 available at that time. It was agreed that the remaining £4,000 should be raised by the issue of State £1 notes, 1,500 of which should be payable in April 1817, 1,250 in October the same year, and 1,250 in April 1818.

... The success of this first creation of State money was so great that it was rapidly followed by others. In June 1819 the question of the market became ever more acute, and it was agreed to finance the rebuilding of it, not in the orthodox manner by raising a loan, but by the State creating the necessary notes "interest free".

On 29th March 1826 a further issue was authorized to re-build Elizabeth College and some parochial schools.

... The experiment continued over a period of 20 years, by which time the people of Guernsey had developed from a depressed unhappy state to a position of prosperity and happiness. And so it went on until £55,000 had been issued as notes. The success being due in no small part to the great care with which the quantity of money to be issued was considered by the States.

... As a result of these "experiments" very tangible benefits were felt by the islanders in the form of the brand new Market House, a refurbished Elizabeth College, better roads and a modern sewage system; all of which were constructed without a debt being incurred by the community."

Today, according to Wikipedia,

"Guernsey does not have a Central Bank and it issues its own sterling coinage and banknotes. U.K. coinage and banknotes also circulate freely and interchangeably. Individuals resident in the Jurisdiction of Guernsey pay income tax at the rate of 20 per cent on their worldwide income. Guernsey levies no capital gains, inheritance, capital transfer, value added (VAT) or general withholding taxes. From 1 January 2008 it has operated a Zero-Ten corporate tax system where most companies pay 0 per cent corporate tax and a limited number of activities are subject to taxation, including banking activity (taxed at 10 per cent), regulated utilities and income from the sale of land or building (taxed at 20 per cent)."

Money Created by the Bank of North Dakota

North Dakota is a state in the Midwestern and northern regions of the United States. It is the 19th most extensive, but the 4th least populous, and the 4th most sparsely populated of the 50 U.S. states. North Dakota was admitted as the 39th state to the Union on November 2, 1889. The state capital is Bismarck, and the largest city is Fargo.

During the early 1900s, North Dakota's economy was based on agriculture, specifically wheat. Frequent drought and harsh winters did not make it easy to earn a living. The arduous growing season was further complicated by grain dealers outside the state who suppressed grain prices, farm suppliers who increased their prices, and banks in Minneapolis and Chicago which raised the interest rates on farm loans, sometimes up to 12 per cent. In an endeavour to improve the financial situation of the state, the Bank of North Dakota was established by legislative action in 1919 to promote agriculture, commerce and industry in North Dakota. This state was the only one of the 48 states that in 1919 accepted the government offer of setting up their own state banks.

According to Wikipedia,

> "North Dakota is the fastest-growing state in U.S. by GDP. Its growth rate is about 8.3 per cent. The economy of North Dakota had a gross domestic product of $36.8 billion in 2013. The per capita income in 2013 was $50,899, ranked 16th in the nation. ...As of May 2014, the state's unemployment rate is the lowest in the U.S at 2.6 per cent. It has not reached 5 percent since 1987. At end of 2010, the state per capita income was ranked 17th in the U.S., the biggest increase of any state in a decade from rank 38th."

The state Bank of North Dakota is at the root of the economic success of this state. The state and its agencies are required to place their funds in the bank, but local governments are not required to do so. The deposits are guaranteed by the general fund of the state of North Dakota itself and the taxpayers of the state. The bank also guarantees student loans (through its Student Loans of North Dakota division), business development loans, and state and municipal bonds

With regard to the kind of money that is used or created by the state bank, it is illuminating to see the following excerpts of an article by Ellen Brown about the state Bank of North Dakota.

According to Ellen Brown's article *"Turning the Tables on Wall Street: North Dakota Shows Cash-starved States how They can Create Their Own Credit"*[10],

"...Still, you may ask, how does that solve the solvency problem? Isn't the state limited to spending only the money it has? The answer is no. Certified, card-carrying bankers are allowed to do something nobody else can do: they can create "credit" with accounting entries on their books.

The Federal Reserve's 10 percent reserve requirement is now largely obsolete, in part because banks have figured out how to get around it with such games as "overnight sweeps". What chiefly limits bank lending today is the 8 percent capital requirement imposed by the Bank for International Settlements, the head of the private global central banking system in Basel, Switzerland. With an 8 percent capital requirement, a state with its own bank could fan its revenues into 12.5 times their face value in loans (100 / 8 = 12.5). And since the state would actually own the bank, it would not have to worry about shareholders or profits. It could lend to credit-worthy borrowers at very low interest, perhaps limited only to a service charge covering its costs; and it could lend to itself or to its municipal governments at as low as zero percent interest. If these loans were rolled over indefinitely, the effect would be the same as creating new, debt-free money.

But, you ask, wouldn't that be dangerously inflationary? Not if the money were used to create new goods and services. Price inflation results only when "demand" (money) exceeds "supply" (goods and services). When they increase together, prices remain stable.

...Our workers and our factories are sitting idle because the private credit system has failed. An injection of new money

---

10   Brown, 2009

from a system of public banks could thaw the credit freeze and bring spring to the markets again. The mathematical flaw in the private credit system is the enormous tribute siphoned off to private coffers in the form of interest. A public banking system could overcome that flaw by returning the interest to the public purse. This is the sort of banking that was pioneered in Benjamin Franklin's colony of Pennsylvania, where it worked brilliantly well. We need to return to our historical roots and implement that system again."

Thus, although the money created by this state bank is in principle unsound fiat money, because it is created by means of fractional reserve banking, it may approach the condition of sound money provided it is correctly used by the state, as indicated in the article. However, the problem remains that the nation's central bank, the Federal Reserve, is not questioned and the monetary system continues to work untouched.

Money in The BRICS Countries

The BRICS acronym stands for the following countries, Brazil, Russia, India, China and South Africa. In connexion with these countries, it is illustrative to read the following excerpt taken from the book by Ellen Brown *The Public Bank Solution: From Austerity to Prosperity*[11].

"Today, the BRIC bloc is evolving into not just an economic but a political force, and under-girding it all is a strong public banking sector. Brazil and Russia, the first two countries in the BRIC acronym, are both forging bright futures with public banks as key features of their economies. Brazil is considered the most successful model among the BRICs, while Russia is expected to be the richest country in Europe by 2030."

---

11   Brown, 2013

The BRIC group have become an alliance with Russia as the main driving force. They became a formal organization in 2009. In 2010, South Africa joined the group at China's invitation.

The BRICS want, among other things, to create an alternative to the dollar as the world reserve currency. The major driving force of the economies of the BRICS is their strong public banking sectors.

In Russia, bank ownership is going from private to public according to a 2009 paper by the Federal Reserve Bank of St. Louis titled *Russian Banking: The State Makes a Comeback*, in which one can read:

> "Concentration is increasing within the public sector of the industry, with the top five state-controlled banking groups in possession of over 49 per cent of assets. We observe a crowding out and erosion of domestic private capital, whose market share is shrinking from year to year. Several of the largest state-owned banks now constitute a de facto intermediate tier at the core of the banking system."

The Asian crisis of 1998 and the banking crisis of 2008 caused many Russians to lose their savings in private banks, thus creating a distrust of these banks. This, together with global financial uncertainty and economic independence, is the reason why Russia is expected to continue with state-owned banks dominating the banking industry for the foreseeable future.

As regards China, the Chinese government owns the banks and many of its enterprises. At the root of China's economic success is the Japanese model of "state-guided" capitalism. In China, a strong public banking sector functions as a major tool of the central government's industrial policy. Because of the control of the Chinese government over its banks, China was able to keep credit flowing during the 2008 banking crisis, while the United States and many other countries were trapped in a bank created credit crunch.

In 2003, Luiz Inacio Lula da Silva (Lula) became Brazil's president. During his eight years in office, he achieved some spectacular successes. He paid off Brazil's debts and transformed Brazil's currency, the Real, into one of the world's strongest currencies. Brazil even became in 2009 an IMF creditor.

Lula rescued his country from insolvency by using financial institutions owned by the government, notably the National Economic and Social Development Bank (BNDES), to finance many credit-worthy projects like road construction, dam building, bridge building, mining companies, etc.

Dedollarization

In this section, we will address the question of the possible end of the U.S. dollar as reserve currency. In this respect, we think that the following article titled *Suddenly, "De-Dollarization" Is A Thing*, authored by John Rubino via DollarCollapse.com, that appeared in *Zerohedge*[12] is very illustrative. For this reason, we give the article in full.

> "For what seems like decades, other countries have been tiptoeing away from their dependence on the US dollar.
>
> China, Russia, and India have cut deals in which they agree to accept each others' currencies for bi-lateral trade while Europe, obviously, designed the euro to be a reserve asset and international medium of exchange.
>
> These were challenges to the dollar's dominance, but they weren't mortal threats.
>
> What's happening lately, however, is a lot more serious.

---

12   Rubino, 2017

It even has an ominous-sounding name: de-dollarization. Here's an excerpt from a much longer article by "strategic risk consultant" F. William Engdahl:

Gold, Oil and De-Dollarization? Russia and China's Extensive Gold Reserves, China Yuan Oil Market (Global Research)

China, increasingly backed by Russia—the two great Eurasian nations—are taking decisive steps to create a very viable alternative to the tyranny of the US dollar over world trade and finance. Wall Street and Washington are not amused, but they are powerless to stop it.

So long as Washington dirty tricks and Wall Street machinations were able to create a crisis such as they did in the Eurozone in 2010 through Greece, world trading surplus countries like China, Japan and then Russia, had no practical alternative but to buy more US Government debt—Treasury securities—with the bulk of their surplus trade dollars. Washington and Wall Street could print endless volumes of dollars backed by nothing more valuable than F-16s and Abrams tanks. China, Russia and other dollar bond holders in truth financed the US wars that were aimed at them, by buying US debt. Then they had few viable alternative options.

Viable Alternative Emerges

Now, ironically, two of the foreign economies that allowed the dollar an artificial life extension beyond 1989—Russia and China—are carefully unveiling that most feared alternative, a viable, gold-backed international currency and potentially, several similar currencies that can displace the unjust hegemonic role of the dollar today.

For several years both the Russian Federation and the Peoples' Republic of China have been buying huge volumes of gold, largely to add to their central bank currency reserves which otherwise are typically in dollars or Euro currencies. Until recently it was not clear quite why.

For several years it's been known in gold markets that the largest buyers of physical gold were the central banks of China and of Russia. What was not so clear was how deep a strategy they had beyond simply creating trust in the currencies amid increasing economic sanctions and bellicose words of trade war out of Washington.

Now it's clear why.

China and Russia, joined most likely by their major trading partner countries in the BRICS (Brazil, Russia, India, China, South Africa), as well as by their Eurasian partner countries of the Shanghai Cooperation Organization (SCO) are about to complete the working architecture of a new monetary alternative to a dollar world.

Currently, in addition to founding members China and Russia, the SCO full members include Kazakhstan, Kyrgyzstan, Tajikistan, Uzbekistan, and most recently India and Pakistan. This is a population of well over 3 billion people, some 42 per cent of the entire world population, coming together in a coherent, planned, peaceful economic and political cooperation.

Gold-Backed Silk Road

It's clear that the economic diplomacy of China, as of Russia and her Eurasian Economic Union group of countries, is very much about realization of advanced high-speed rail, ports, energy infrastructure weaving together a vast new market that, within less than a decade at present pace, will overshadow any economic potentials in the debt-bloated economically stagnant OECD countries of the EU and North America.

What until now was vitally needed, but not clear, was a strategy to get the nations of Eurasia free from the dollar and from their vulnerability to further US Treasury sanctions and financial warfare based on their dollar dependence. This is now about to happen.

At the September 5 annual BRICS Summit in Xiamen, China, Russian President Putin made a simple and very clear statement of the Russian view of the present economic world. He stated, "Russia shares the BRICS countries' concerns over the unfairness of the global financial and economic architecture, which does not give due regard to the growing weight of the emerging economies. We are ready to work together with our partners to promote international financial regulation reforms and to overcome the excessive domination of the limited number of reserve currencies."

To my knowledge he has never been so explicit about currencies. Put this in context of the latest financial architecture unveiled by Beijing, and it becomes clear the world is about to enjoy new degrees of economic freedom.

China Yuan Oil Futures

According to a report in the Japan Nikkei Asian Review, China is about to launch a crude oil futures contract denominated in Chinese Yuan that will be convertible into gold. This, when coupled with other moves over the past two yearsm where China seeks to become a viable alternative to London and New York.

China is the world's largest importer of oil, the vast majority of it still paid in US dollars. If the new Yuan oil futures contract gains wide acceptance, it could become the most important Asia-based crude oil benchmark, given that China is the world's biggest oil importer. That would challenge the two Wall Street-dominated oil benchmark contracts in North

Sea Brent and West Texas Intermediate oil futures that until now has given Wall Street huge hidden advantages.

That would be one more huge manipulation lever eliminated by China and its oil partners, including very specially Russia. Introduction of an oil futures contract traded in Shanghai in Yuan, which recently gained membership in the select IMF SDR group of currencies, oil futures especially when convertible into gold, could change the geopolitical balance of power dramatically away from the Atlantic world to Eurasia.

In April 2016 China made a major move to become the new centre for gold exchange and the world centre of gold trade, physical gold. China today is the world's largest gold producer, far ahead of fellow BRICS member South Africa, with Russia number two.

Now to add the new oil futures contract traded in China in Yuan with the gold backing will lead to a dramatic shift by key OPEC members, even in the Middle East, to prefer gold-backed Yuan for their oil over inflated US dollars that carry a geopolitical risk as Qatar experienced following the Trump visit to Riyadh some months ago. Notably, Russian state oil giant, Rosneft just announced that Chinese state oil company, CEFC China Energy Company Ltd, just bought a 14 per cent share of Rosneft from Qatar. It's all beginning to fit together into a very coherent strategy. Meanwhile, in Latin America:

De-Dollarization Spikes – Venezuela Stops Accepting Dollars For Oil Payments (Zero Hedge)

Did the doomsday clock on the petrodollar (and implicitly US hegemony) just tick one more minute closer to midnight?

Apparently confirming what President Maduro had warned following the recent US sanctions, The *Wall Street Journal* reports that Venezuela has officially stopped accepting US

Dollars as payment for its crude oil exports.

As we previously noted, Venezuelan President Nicolas Maduro said last Thursday that Venezuela will be looking to "free" itself from the U.S. dollar next week. According to Reuters, "Venezuela is going to implement a new system of international payments and will create a basket of currencies to free us from the dollar," Maduro said in a multi-hour address to a new legislative "super-body." He reportedly did not provide details of this new proposal.

Maduro hinted further that the South American country would look to using the yuan instead, among other currencies.

"If they pursue us with the dollar, we'll use the Russian Ruble, the Yuan, yen, the Indian Rupee, the Euro," Maduro also said.

The state oil company Petróleos de Venezuela SA, known as PdVSA, has told its private joint venture partners to open accounts in Euros and to convert existing cash holdings into Europe's main currency, said one project partner. This first step towards one or more gold-backed Eurasian currencies certainly looks like a viable and — for a lot of big players out there — welcome addition to the global money stock.

Venezuela, meanwhile illustrates the growing perception of US weakness. It used to be that a small country refusing to take dollars could expect regime change in short order. Now, maybe not so much.

Combine the above with the emergence of bitcoin and its kin as the preferred monetary asset of techies and libertarians, and the monetary world suddenly looks downright multi-polar."

The following article titled *"The Only Russia Story That Matters"*, authored by the lawyer and best seller financial author Jim

Rickards[13], also deals with dedollarization and gives some interesting clues. For this reason, we give the article in full.

"The World Gold Council has reported that the Central Bank of Russia has more than doubled the pace of its gold purchases, bringing its reserves to the highest level since Putin took power 17 years ago.

Russia's desire to break away from the hegemony of the U.S. dollar and the dollar payment system is well-known. Over 60 per cent of global reserves and 80 per cent of global payments are in dollars. The U.S. is the only country with veto power at the International Monetary Fund, the global lender of last resort.

Perhaps Russia's most aggressive weapon in its war on dollars is gold. The first line of defence is to acquire physical gold, which cannot be frozen out of the international payments system or hacked.

With gold, you can always pay another country just by putting the gold on an air-plane and shipping it to the counter-party. This is the 21st-century equivalent of how J.P. Morgan settled payments in gold by ship or rail-road in the early 20th century.

Russia has now tripled its gold reserves from around 600 tonnes to 1,800 tonnes over the past 10 years and shows no signs of slowing down. Even when oil prices and Russian reserves were collapsing in 2015, Russia continued to acquire gold.

But Russia is pursuing other dollar alternatives besides gold. For one, it's been building non-dollar payments systems with regional trading partners and China.

The U.S. uses its influence at SWIFT, the central nervous system of global money transfer message traffic, to cut off

---

13   Rickards, 2017

nations it considers to be threats. From a financial perspective, this is like cutting off oxygen to a patient in the intensive care unit. Russia understands its vulnerability to U.S. domination and wants to reduce that vulnerability.

Now Russia has created an alternative to SWIFT. The head of Russia's central bank, Elvira Nabiullina, has reported to Vladimir Putin that "There was the threat of being shut out of SWIFT. We updated our transaction system, and if anything happens, all SWIFT-format operations will continue to work. We created an analogous system."

Russia is also part of a reported Chinese plan to install a new international monetary order that excludes U.S. dollars. Under that plan, China could buy Russian oil with Yuan and Russia could then exchange that Yuan for gold on the Shanghai exchange. Now it appears Russia has another weapon in its anti-dollar arsenal.

Russia's development bank, VEB, and several Russian state ministries are reportedly teaming up to develop blockchain technology. They want to create a fully encrypted, distributed, inexpensive payments system that does not rely on Western banks, SWIFT or the U.S. to move money around.

This has nothing to do with bitcoin, which is just another digital token. The blockchain technology (now often referred to as distributed ledger technology, or DLT) is a platform that can facilitate a wide variety of transfers — possibly including a new Russian-state cryptocurrency backed by gold.

"Putin coins," anyone?

The ultimate loser here will be the dollar. That's one more reason for investors to allocate part of their portfolios to assets such as gold."

Chapter VII

How to Break Free From the Present Monetary System

We begin this chapter with three quotes on the concept of money.

"Money exists not by nature but by law." — Aristotle

"a money token for purposes of exchange." — Plato

"What is commonly understood as money has always consisted, tangibly, of a number of pieces of some material, marked by public authority and named or understood in the laws or customs: that its palpable characteristic was its mark of authority; its essential characteristic, the possession of value, defined by law; and its function, the legal power to pay debts and taxes and the mechanical power to facilitate the exchange of other objects possessing value." — Alexander del Mar[1]

It is easily seen that our definition of sound (fiat) money given in Chapter 2 essentially coincides with that of del Mar. However, we are more specific as to what gives money its value. We think it is human labour, and that is why we include this characteristic explicitly in our definition of sound money. In this way, we believe that there is no ambiguity as to what sound money is.

In this chapter, we will present a solution to the problems caused by our present monetary system, which have been described in the previous chapters.

---

1   del Mar, 1885, p.2

The 100 per Cent Reserve Solution

Frederick Soddy[2], the 1921 Nobel Prize winner in chemistry, also studied economics and introduced great clarity of thought to the problem of banking panics. In fact, he invented the 100 per cent reserve solution, which is not to be confused with the mere requirement of 100 per cent reserves in commercial banks.

Under the 100 per cent reserve solution, the Treasury would first loan newly created money, out of nothing and free of interest and debt, to the commercial banks to bring their cash reserves up to 100 per cent. The banks would pay interest to the State on these loans. Then, the Central Bank would also borrow from the treasury sufficient new currency to bring its cash reserves up to 100 per cent of its demand deposits. The amount of State securities held by the Central Bank and the commercial banks should be credited against these borrowings, thus cancelling all bonds in existence.

With this elegant plan, all the debt generated by unsound fiat money in existence due to the magic of fractional reserve banking, would be transformed into legal tender money and, as mentioned earlier, all bonds held by the banking system would disappear. Commercial banks would be required to maintain 100 per cent reserves, thus making it impossible that bank runs may happen. It would be impossible for commercial banks and the Central Bank to create money. Only the State would be able to issue money, interest free and without debt. As long as the State could issue money in exchange for goods and services, no inflation would be generated. Commercial banks would get their funds from shares, time deposits or debentures. If a commercial bank goes bankrupt, the State would not bail it out. Thus, commercial banks would operate like any other business.

In August 2012 two researchers at the International Monetary

---

2   Soddy, 1933

Fund, Jaromir Benes and Michael Kumhoff, wrote a working paper titled *The Chicago Plan Revisited*[3], in which they summarized the history of the plan.

"The Chicago Plan provides an outline for the transition from a system of privately-issued debt-based money to a system of government-issued debt-free money. The history of the Chicago Plan is explained in Phillips (1994). It was first formulated in the United Kingdom by the 1921 Nobel Prize winner in chemistry, Frederick Soddy, in Soddy (1926). Professor Frank Knight of the University of Chicago picked up the idea almost immediately, in Knight (1927). The first, March 1933 version of the plan is a memorandum to President Roosevelt (Knight (1933)). Many of Knight's distinguished University of Chicago colleagues supported the plan and signed the memorandum, including especially Henry Simons, who was the author of the second, more detailed memorandum to Roosevelt in November 1933 (Simons et al. (1933). The Chicago economists, and later Irving Fisher of Yale, were in constant contact with the Roosevelt administration, which seriously considered their proposals, as reflected for example in the government memoranda of Gardiner Means (1933) and Lauchlin Currie (1934), and the bill of Senator Bronson Cutting."[4]

They concluded that the plan would successfully solve many of the social and economic problems that our present monetary system causes. In particular, they found that full employment would be the result, business cycles would be abolished and inflation would be close to zero. We cite their conclusion in full.

"This paper revisits the Chicago Plan, a proposal for fundamental monetary reform that was put forward by many leading U.S. economists at the height of the Great Depression.

---

3   Benes and Kumhoff, 2012

4   see Cutting (1934).

Fisher (1936), in his brilliant summary of the Chicago Plan, claimed that it had four major advantages, ranging from greater macroeconomic stability to much lower debt levels throughout the economy. In this paper we are able to rigorously evaluate his claims, by applying the recommendations of the Chicago Plan to a state-of-the-art monetary DSGE model that contains a fully micro-founded and carefully calibrated model of the current U.S. financial system. The critical feature of this model is that the economy's money supply is created by banks, through debt, rather than being created debt-free by the government.

Our analytical and simulation results fully validate Fisher's (1936) claims. The Chicago Plan could significantly reduce business cycle volatility caused by rapid changes in banks' attitudes towards credit risk, it would eliminate bank runs, and it would lead to an instantaneous and large reduction in the levels of both government and private debt. It would accomplish the latter by making government-issued money, which represents equity in the commonwealth rather than debt, the central liquid asset of the economy, while banks concentrate on their strength, the extension of credit to investment projects that require monitoring and risk management expertise. We find that the advantages of the Chicago Plan go even beyond those claimed by Fisher. One additional advantage is large steady state output gains due to the removal or reduction of multiple distortions, including interest rate risk spreads, distortionary taxes, and costly monitoring of macro-economically unnecessary credit risks. Another advantage is the ability to drive steady state inflation to zero in an environment where liquidity traps do not exist, and where monetarism becomes feasible and desirable because the government does in fact control broad monetary aggregates. This ability to generate and live with zero steady state inflation is an important result, because it answers the somewhat confused claim of opponents of an exclusive government monopoly on money issuance, namely that such a monetary system would be highly inflationary. There is nothing in our theoretical framework to support this claim. And as discussed in Section II, there is very little in the monetary history of ancient societies and Western nations to support it either. "

Solutions for Some Countries in the Euro Area

In the case of present time Europe, the Chicago plan, mentioned in the previous section, would be the optimal solution. However, even if the Chicago plan is not globally implemented, individual countries in the European Monetary Union make take some action to remedy the painful situation in which they are trapped.

The second solution would be to implement a local version of the Chicago plan. More specifically, we propose that the State in question, for example, Spain, issues its own money, free of interest and debt, as a parallel sound fiat currency.

This new currency, called for example the SEuro, would be declared legal tender and would be accepted in payment of taxes and debts.

Banks would be allowed to open deposit accounts in the new currency, but they would be forced to have 100 per cent reserves in that currency. That is, no fractional reserve banking would be allowed in SEuros. Commercial banks would not be permitted to create SEuros out of nothing.

The government would introduce the new SEuros through a spending program in infrastructure, hospitals, housing, schools, and other needed social interventions. The officials at the Central Bank would be in charge to guarantee that the money is properly spent. This would prevent the generation of inflation and would ensure that sound fiat money is generated.

The parity between the usual Euro and the SEuro would be at the beginning 1:1. In the course of time, the market would establish a different parity.

The previous plan would generate employment under a noninflationary environment. It would also prevent the generation of more debt. Moreover, the existing debt could be repaid overtime.

The two currencies would coexist, but only Euros would be allowed for payments abroad. SEuros would be used inside Spain exclusively.

The amount of SEuros to be issued by the State would be determined by the economic needs of the country. Once the optimum level is arrived, no more issuance would be needed. Only if there is economic and demographic growth, or in case of war, the supply of SEuros would be increased adequately.

Given that the two previous solutions may be difficult to implement, due to the resistance that will be expected on the part of the power elite if there is a move in that direction, we still propose a third solution.

This third solution is not as good as the other two in our opinion, but at least it would be an improvement over the current situation and, more importantly, it would be completely legal. It would not be necessary to change the existing European treaties. The solution consists of creating a state bank in the reference country, similar to the Bank of North Dakota, mentioned in Chapter 6, with respect to the U.S.

For example, a state owned bank in Spain could provide credit to the country itself for infrastructure projects, help provide the capital for local commercial banks, so they could in turn provide low interest loans to home owners, small and medium sized businesses, and students. In addition, a state bank could be used to help fund state expenses during tough times by providing loans.

A major advantage of a state bank is that the country could borrow money from the bank at zero interest for projects, saving between 50 per cent and 100 per cent of the cost of the project, since there would be no interest burden when repaying the loan. For Greece, Spain, Italy, and other countries looking to solve their economic problems, the state bank model should be studied in depth, as such a bank could provide the credit needed within that country economy during depressions and other tough economic times.

As mentioned in Chapter 6, extreme care should be used when implementing a state bank in a certain country, in the sense that the money should be correctly used so as to foster real economic activity in a noninflationary environment.

Chapter VIII

Epilogue

In the previous chapters, we have explained how the present monetary system works and we have exposed its disastrous consequences on many aspects of our society. One of them is the complete lack of criticism, with very few exceptions, in academia or the mainstream media with respect to this subject. One exception is provided by the interview published in the Spanish newspaper *El Mundo* on March 5th, 2017, with the prestigious economist Arthur B. Laffer, creator of the famous Laffer curve representing the relationship between rates of taxation and the resulting levels of government revenue, where he concluded:

> "Economists select their research topics according to political criteria, and they deny the truth of things they know are true whenever it suits them in order to get political favours. The same thing happens in the U.S., in Germany and in Spain. I do not accept money from politicians."

As another exception, we can cite the following excerpt that corresponds to the article by Brett Maverick Musser titled *Energy, Money and the Destruction of Equilibrium*,[1] published on the *Zerohedge* web page.

> "To paraphrase Paul Romer author of the scathing paper "The Trouble With Macro" (see Romer, 2016), economics has had a 'considerable observed regression since the 1970s' yet hides behind mathematical elegance and authority that the public at large is not sophisticated enough to rebuke nor powerful enough to eschew. Never ending zero interest rate policies,

---

1   Musser, 2017

negative interest rates and other forms of financial alchemy perpetuated by central banks all over the world are intellectual concessions that the existing paradigm of economic thought and authority is just flat wrong. No matter what the economic leaders say, these actions prove to me and many others that their mental models of the world have failed. The status quo has ventured into the shallow sea of un-reason just to keep the global socio-economic system afloat. They're able to hide behind authority and academic vocabulary which if put in plain terms for the lay person could be described as theft, ponzi, tyrannical and moronic."

In this Epilogue we will address the question as to what is the situation nowadays, where we are heading and whether there is still time to change things for the better.

In a speech at the National Economists Club given in November 2002 and titled *Deflation: making sure "it" doesn't happen here* [2], the former Governor of the Federal Reserve Ben Bernanke detailed all the measures that the Fed could take in the future in order to avoid deflation. Did Bernanke know that a housing bubble was coming and that when it popped in 2008 a recession followed by a deflation would ensue? We can only guess, but the fact is that Bernanke presented a series of measures to prevent deflation that would be later implemented by the Federal Reserve as if it followed a road map (prophecy?) that had been previously written.

But before we go into the details of Bernanke's speech, let us review some background information on central banks and the situation back in 2002. First of all, the language used by central bankers is unduly complex, as if they did not want ordinary people to understand what they have to say about economics, when in reality what they have to say is rather simple. So, our first task will be to present Bernanke's proposals in plain language so that everybody can understand what he said.

---

2   Bernanke, 2002

Deflation can be defined as a contraction of the money supply. Usually this contraction causes a recession. Remember, for example, the Great Depression described in Chapter 5, that was caused by a severe deflation after the stock market crash.

Bernanke probably knew in 2002 what was coming with regard to indebtedness growing bigger and bigger. The bubble that was forming would burst someday and he wanted to have a plan to avoid, or at least attenuate, the drastic consequences of the ensuing recession. In other words, he did not want a repetition of the Great Depression of 1929 that had unleashed havoc in the U.S. In his own words:

"However, a deflationary recession may differ in one respect from "normal" recessions in which the inflation rate is at least modestly positive: Deflation of sufficient magnitude may result in the nominal interest rate declining to zero or very close to zero. Once the nominal interest rate is at zero, no further downward adjustment in the rate can occur, since lenders generally will not accept a negative nominal interest rate when it is possible instead to hold cash. At this point, the nominal interest rate is said to have hit the "zero bound." "

He is telling us that, because the interest rate is zero or close to zero, the central bank can no longer use its usual monetary instrument, the interest rate, to generate inflation. However, that does not mean that the central bank has run out of options. On the contrary, he continues:

"We conclude that, under a paper-money system, a determined government can always generate higher spending and hence positive inflation."

The following is a list of all the measures that he proposed to take to avoid deflation and whether they were actually taken after 2008 or not.

Zero Interest Rate Policy	done
Expand asset purchases	done
Print money	done
Expand menu of assets	done
Buy real and financial assets	done
Buy private assets	done
Tax cuts and rebates	not yet

Thus, the only measure not taken yet is that of tax cuts and rebates. This would mean in his words:

"A money-financed tax cut is essentially equivalent to Milton Friedman's famous "helicopter drop" of money."

Another measure not implemented yet is that of banning cash, although Bernanke hinted at it when he said:

"lenders generally will not accept a negative nominal interest rate when it is possible instead to hold cash."

Since we are living in an environment of negative interest rates, as shown in the picture on the next page, we should be prepared for a ban in cash. Indeed, as shown in Chapter 5, economists are already trying to convince us that this is a good idea. Now we know the reason.

After the burst of the housing bubble in 2008, the Fed started to implement all of the previous measures to mitigate the consequences of the depression. We can summarize the Fed's behaviour by saying that it has been injecting huge amounts of money into the top of the wealth pyramid, as explained in Chapter 5, to prevent many banks and powerful firms from going bankrupt. But, by bailing them out, the market has not been able to perform its function of cleaning and returning to equilibrium and consequently people no longer know which

banks and institutions are sound and which are n~~r~~
called zombie economic situation. On the othe~~·~~
money created by our system is based on debt, a deb~~ι~~ ~
been created. Since debt is accompanied by interest that p~~eu,~~
must pay with taxes, this enormous debt creation impoverishes
the people. In fact, Assurant's CEO, Alan Colberg, stated on
March 6th, 2017, that:

> "The reality is, half of Americans can't afford to write a $500
> check."

The effect of people getting poorer plus demographic effects, like
the baby boomers heading into retirement, will eventually cause
a deflation. Until then, there will be an unstable equilibrium
between deflation and inflation with the people progressively
getting poorer. In case a severe deflation sets in, the Fed's last
cartridge will be to give helicopter money directly to the people in
the form of tax cuts and rebates, the last of Bernanke's measures
not taken yet. But this will probably cause a hyperinflation.

How long can we be in this unstable situation until a severe
deflation sets in? Nobody knows, it depends on the rate of
impoverishment of the people. In Japan they have been in
this unstable situation with low deflation for twenty years and
counting.

Another question is why we have negative interest rates. The
reason is to keep the debt service under control, because all those
quantitative easing episodes have pushed the debt service out of
control. But if you have negative interest rates, you lose money
and that is the reason why they want to outlaw cash. They want
the people to either have money in the bank or spend it. In this
way, they think that they will be able to generate inflation while
maintaining the debt service under control.

One point that we have not addressed yet is that of the effect
that automation will have on the economy in the future. In this

pect, we refer the reader to the following excerpt of an article
y Ben Tarnoff titled *Robots won't just take our jobs – they'll make
the rich even richer*, published on line by the *theguardian*[3].

"What's different this time is the possibility that technology
will become so sophisticated that there won't be anything left
for humans to do. What if your ATM could not only give you
a hundred bucks, but sell you an adjustable-rate mortgage?
While the current rhetoric around artificial intelligence
is over-hyped, there have been meaningful advances over
the past several years. And it's not inconceivable that much
bigger breakthroughs are on the horizon. Instead of merely
transforming work, technology might begin to eliminate it.
Instead of making it possible to create more wealth with less
labour, automation might make it possible to create more
wealth *without* labour.

What's so bad about wealth without labour? It depends on
who owns the wealth. Under capitalism, wages are how
workers receive a portion of what they produce. That portion
has always been small, relative to the rewards that flow to
the owners of capital. And over the past several decades, it's
gotten smaller: the share of the national income that goes to
wages has been steadily shrinking, while the share that goes
to capital has been growing. Technology has made workers
more productive, but the profits have trickled up, not down.
Productivity increased by 80.4% between 1973 and 2011, but
the real hourly compensation of the median worker went up
by only 10.7%...

Job-killing robots are good, in other words, so long as the
prosperity they produce is widely distributed. An Oxfam
report released earlier this year revealed that the eight richest
men in the world own as much wealth as half the human race.
Imagine what those numbers will look like if automation

---

3   Tarnoff, 2017

accelerates. At some point, a handful of billionaires could control close to one hundred percent of society's wealth. Then, perhaps, the idea that wealth should be owned by the many, rather than monopolized by the few, won't seem so radical, and we can undertake a bit of sorely needed redistribution – before robot capitalism kills us all."

Given the previous considerations, the future does not look bright for the immense majority of mankind. We are running out of time if we want to change things for the better, and we think that a precondition for it is to change the present monetary system. This system is unjust, immoral and inefficient and if we do not change it we will sooner than later have a society in which a very small, immensely rich, elite will have complete control over the rest of an impoverished mankind.

Appendix

Letter from President Abraham Lincoln written in December 1864 to Colonel E.D. Taylor concerning the Greenbacks.

Chicago Illinois

Colonel E D Taylor

I have long determined to make public the origin of the greenback and tell the world that it is one of Dick Taylor's creations. You had always been friendly to me, and when troublous times fell upon us, and my shoulders, though broad and willing, were weak, and myself surrounded by such circumstances and such people that I knew not whom to trust, then I said in my extremity, "I will send for Colonel Taylor; he will know what to do." I think it was in January 1862, on or about the 16th, that I did so. You came, and I said to you, "What shall we do?" Said you, "Why, issue treasure notes bearing no interest, printed on the best banking paper. Issue enough to pay off the army expenses, and declare it legal tender." Chase thought it a hazardous thing, but we finally accomplished it, and gave to the people of this Republic the greatest blessing they ever had – their own paper to pay off their own debts. It is due to you, the father of the present greenback, that the people should know it, and I take great pleasure in making it known. How many times I have laughed at you telling me plainly that I was too lazy to be anything but a lawyer.

Yours truly A Lincoln

This hand written letter was verified and documented on February 10, 1888 by the 50th United States Congress.

Appendix

We also present in this Appendix the text, in the original German with translation into English, of part of a speech given by Adolf Hitler on February 20, 1938, in which he addresses the question of the role that money should take in Germany at the time.

"Es wird auch in der Zukunft unsere Aufgabe sein, das deutsche Volk vor allen Illusionen zu bewahren. Die schlimmste Illusion ist aber immer die, zu glauben, daß man etwas erleben kann, was vorher nicht durch Arbeit geschaffen und produziert wurde.

Es wird auch in der Zukunft unsere Pflicht sein, jedem einzelnen Deutschen in Stadt und Land klarzumachen, daß der Wert seiner Arbeit stets gleich bleiben muß seinem Lohn.

Das heißt, Der Bauer kann für seine Landprodukte nur das bekommen, was der Städter vorher erarbeitet hat, und der Städter kann nur erhalten was der Bauer seinem Boden abrang, und alle untereinander können nur austauschen, als sie produzieren, und das Geld kann dabei nur die Mittlerrolle spielen.

Es trägt keinen eigenen Gebrauchswert in sich. Jede Mark, die in Deutschland mehr bezahlt wird, setzt voraus, daß um eine Mark mehr gearbeitet wurde. Ansonsten ist diese Mark ein leeres Stück Papier, daß keine Kaufkraft besitzt.

Wir aber wollen, daß unsere deutsche Reichsmark ein ehrlicher Schein bleibt, eine ehrliche Ausweisung für das Produkt einer von einem anderen ebenso ehrlich geleisteten Arbeit.

Dies ist die wahre, weil einzige und wirkliche Deckung einer Währung. Dadurch haben wir es ermöglicht, ohne Gold und ohne Devisen den Wert der deutschen Mark zu erhalten, und haben damit auch der Wert unserer Sparguthaben sichergestellt zu einer Zeit, da jene Länder die von Gold un Devisen überlaufen, ihre Währungen selbst entwerten mußten.

Schon der Geburtssegen wird uns zwingen, durch Erh¨ohung unserer Produktion das erh¨ohte Auskommen fu¨r die Gesamtheit sicherzustellen. Wir haben uns nun in den Jahren 1933/34 gezwungen gesehen, die deutsche Arbeitskraft, um sie u¨berhaupt erst einmal zur Wirkung zu bringen, nicht selten in primitivster Form auszusetzen. Spaten und Schaufel waren in diesen Jahren die Werkzeuge fu¨r viele Hunderttausende deutscher M¨anner. Mit der steigenden Inbetriebsetzung unseres wirtschaftliches Lebens erfolgte eine langsame Umstellung auch in unseren Arbeitsmethoden. Heute leidet Deutschland an einem Mangel gelernter Arbeitskr¨afte. Die Arbeitslosigkeit als solche its so gut wie restlos beseitigt."

English Translation:

"It will also be our task in the future to warn the German people against all kinds of illusions. The worst illusion is to think that one can enjoy something in life that has not been previously created and produced.

It will also be our duty in the future to make clear to all German people, in the city as well as in the land, that the value of their labor is and should always be equal to their salary.

That is, the countryman can only receive for his products what the man in the city has previously produced, and the man in the city can only get what the countryman has previously obtained from his land, and all of them can only make interchanges while they are producing, and money can only play an intermediary role in this process.

Money cannot have an intrinsic value. Each new Mark that is paid in Germany presupposes an additional human labor valued one Mark. Otherwise, this Mark is an empty piece of paper that has no purchasing power.

We want however our Reichsmark to be an honorable banknote,

an honorable receipt for the result of equally honorable human labor.

This is the only real and authentic backing of a currency. In this way we have made it possible, without gold and foreign currencies, to keep the value of the German Mark stable, and we have also kept our savings stable, in times in which those countries that were swimming in gold and foreign currencies had to devalue their currencies.

The birth blessing will force us to ensure that everybody will be sufficiently taken care of through an increase in production. In order to be able to employ the German workers for the first time, we have often been forced in the years 1933/34 to use primitive means. Spades and shovels were the tools in those years for many hundreds of thousands of German men. Our working methods started to change slowly through the increase of our economic activity. Today, Germany suffers from the lack of a skilled labor force. Unemployment has been completely eradicated.

Bibliography

Amadeo, K. (2017, June). What Caused The 2008 Global Financial Crisis? Downloadable at https://www.thebalance.com/what-caused-2008-global-financial-crisis-3306176

Andr´ead`es, A. (1966). History Of The Bank Of England 1640-1903 (fourth ed.). Frank Cass & Co. Ltd.: Abingdon, Oxon.

Benes, J., and Kumhof, M. (2012). The Chicago Plan Revisited. IMF Working Paper WP/12/202.

Bernanke, B. S. (2002, November). Deflation: Making sure "it" doesn't happen here. Downloadable at https://www.federalreserve.gov/boarddocs/speeches/ 2002/20021121/default.htm

Bierman, H. (2008, March). The 1929 Stock Market Crash. Downloadable at http://eh.net/encyclopedia/the-1929-stock-market-crash/

Blanchard, O. (2014, September). Where Danger Lurks. Finance and Development, 51 (3).

Brown, E. H. (2009, March, 11th). Turning The Tables On Wall Street: North Dakota Shows Cash-Starved States How They Can Create Their Own Credit. Downloadable at http://www.webofdebt.com/articles/state bank option2.php

Brown, E. H. (2011, April). Libya: All About Oil, Or All About Banking? Downloadable at www.webofdebt.com/articles/libya.php

Brown, E. H. (2013). The Public Bank Solution: From Austerity To Prosperity. Third Millennium Press: Baton Rouge, Louisiana.

Bibliography

Brzezinski, Z. (1997). The Grand Chessboard: American Primacy And Its Geostrategic Imperatives. Basic Bools: New York.

Coogan, G. M. (1963). Money Creators, Who Creates Money? Who Should Create It? Omni Publications, Hawthorne, California.

Cook, R. C. (2008, July). Louis T. Mcfadden (1876-1936): An American Hero. Downloadable at http://www.pacificfreepress. com/2008/07/29/ opinion/an-american-hero-louis-t-mcfadden-1876-1936.html

del Mar, A. (1885). Money In Ancient Countries. Bell: London.

del Mar, A. (2000). History Of Monetary Systems. University Press of the Pacific: Honolulu, Hawaii.

de Soto, J. H. (2009). Classical Liberalism Versus Anarchocapitalism. In J. G. Hu¨lsmann and S. Kinsella (Eds.), Property, freedom, and society: Essays in honor of hans-hermann hoppe. Ludwig von Mises Institute.

Elliott, L. (2017). World's Eight Richest People Have Same Wealth As Poorest 50%. Downloadable at https://www.theguardian.com/ global-development/2017/jan/16/worlds- eight-richest-people-have-same-wealth-as-poorest-50

Galbraith, J. K. (2001). Money: Whence It Came, Where It Went. Houghton Mifflin: T.

Hall, A. (2010, September). Germany was strong-armed by french into swapping the deutschmark for the euro. Downloadable at http://www.dailymail.co.uk/news/article-1315622/Germany-strong-armed-France-swapping- Deutschmark-euro.html

Hoskins, R. K. (1985). War Cycles - Peace Cycles. The Virginian Publishing Company: Lynchburg, Virginia.

Hugh-Smith, C. (2015). If We Don't Change The Way Money Is Created & Distributed, We Change Nothing. Downloadable at http://www.zerohedge.com/news/2015-12-24/if-we-dont-change-way- money-created-distributed-we-change-nothing

Keynes, J. M. (1920). The Economic Consequences Of The Peace. Harcourt Brace: New York.

Lincoln, A., and Hertz, E. (1931). Abraham lincoln, a new portrait. Horace Liveright Inc.: New York.

Lincoln, A., and Shaw, A. H. (1950). The Lincoln Encyclopedia : The Spoken And Written Words Of A. Lincoln Arranged For Ready Reference. New York: Macmillan.

Litterick, D. (2002, September). Billionaire Who Broke The Bank Of England. Downloadable at http://www.telegraph.co.uk/finance/2773265/Billionaire-who-broke-the-Bank-of-England.html

Luther, D. (2017). What Does The Future Hold For 'Average Joes' ? (spoiler alert: Feudalism). Downloadable at http://www.zerohedge.com/news/2017-01-11/what-does-future-hold-   average-joes-spoiler-alert-feudalism

Maloney, M. (2016). Hidden Secrets Of Money. Downloadable at https://goldsilver.com/blog/the-usas-day-of-reckoning-hidden-secrets-of-money-episode-7/

Marsh, D. (1992). The Bundesbank: The Bank That Rules Europe. William Heinemann Ltd.: London.

McNamara, R. J. (2017). The Black Friday Gold Corner. Downloadable at http://history1800s.about.com/od/robber-barons/ss/Black-Friday- Gold-Corner.htm

Meacham, J. (2008). American Lion: Andrew Jackson In The White House. Random House: New York.

Miaozc. (2015). Jiaozi And Iron Standard – Examining The World's First Documented Paper Money System From China With Lenses On Austrian Economics. Downloadable at http://rothbardiangoldprice.com/2015/08/jiaozi-and-iron-standrad-examining-worlds-first-documented-paper-money-system-from-china-with-lenses-of-austrian-economics/

Mullins, E. (1983). The Secrets Of The Federal Reserve. Bankers Research Institute: Staunton, Virginia.

Musser, B. M. (2017, February). Energy, Money And The Destruction Of Equilibrium. Downloadable at http://www.zerohedge.com/news/2017-02-28/ energy-money-and-destruction-equilibrium

Overy, R. J. (1982). The Nazi Economic Recovery. London: Macmillan. Polleit, T. (2016, May). Cash banned, freedom gone. Downloadable at https://mises.org/library/cash-banned-freedom-gone

Quigley, C. (1966). Tragedy And Hope: A History Of The World In Our Time. The Macmillan Company: New York.

Rickards, J. (2017, October). The Only Russia Story That Matters. Downloadable at https://dailyreckoning.com/russia-story-matters/

Robinson, J. (2012a, December). Preparing For The Collapse Of The Petrodollar System, part 2. Downloadable at https://ftmdaily.com/preparing-for-the- collapse-of-the-petrodollar-part-2/

Robinson, J. (2012b, December). Preparing For The Collapse Of The Petrodollar System, Part 4. Downloadable at http://ftmdaily.com/wp-content/uploads/2012/12/Preparing-for-the-Collapse-of-the-Petrodollar-System-Part-4.pdf

Rogoff, K. S. (2016). The Curse Of Cash. Princeton University Press: Princeton, New Jersey.

Romer, P. (2016, September). The Trouble With Macroeconomics. Downloadable at https://paulromer.net/wp-content/uploads/2016/09/WP-Trouble.pdf

Rubino, J. (2017, September). Suddenly, "de-dollarization" is a thing. Downloadable at http://www.zerohedge.com/news/2017-09-16/suddenly-de- dollarization-thing

Schacht, H. (1967). The Magic of Money. Oldbourne: London.

Search, R. E. (1989). Lincoln Money Martyred. Omni Publications: Palmdate, California.

Silverman, D. P. (1988). National Socialist Economics: The Wirtschaftswunder Reconsidered. In E. B and T. J. Hutton (Eds.), Interwar unemployment in international perspective (p. 185-220.). Kluwer Academic Publishers.

Soddy, F. (1933). Wealth, Virtual Wealth And Debt, The Solution Of The Economic Paradox. Britons Publishing Company: London.

Still, W. T., and Carmack, P. S. (1996). The Money Masters. Downloadable at https://archive.org/stream/TheMoneyMasters/Money_Masters_djvu.txt

Sutton, A. (1981). Wall Street And The Bolshevik Revolution. Arlington House Publishers: New Rochelle, New York.

Tarnoff, B. (2017, March). Robots won't just take our jobs – they'll make the rich even richer. Downloadable at https://www.theguardian.com/technology/2017/mar/02/robot-tax-job- elimination-livable-wage

Villaverde, J. F. (2015, August). Mis Aveturas Con Bitcoin I: El Dinero Es Memoria. Downloadable at http://nadaesgratis.es/fernandez-villaverde/mis-aventuras-con- bitcoin-i-el-dinero-es-memoria

Bibliography

Villaverde, J. F. (2016, September). Eliminemos el dinero (en met´alico). Downloadable at http://nadaesgratis.es/fernandez-villaverde/eliminemos-el-dinero- en-metalico

von Mises, L. (1934). Theory Of Money And Credit. Capetown: J. Cape.

von Mises, L. (1996). Human Action, A Treatise On Economics (fourth ed.). Fox & Wilkes: San Fracisco, CA.

Watson, T. (2011). Sketches from Roman history. The Barnes Review, Washington DC .

Zarlenga, S. A. (2002). Lost Science Of Money, The Mithology Of Money - The Story Of Power. American Monetary Institute.

Contracts   Rate %.   Interest Rate 3m.

Feb: 99.8175 ⎤
Mar: 99.8300 ⎦ 0.9 %.   3m Libor 0.1825

Apr : 99.8400 ⎤
may : 99.8400 ⎦ 1%.   3m Libor 0.16

Jan : 99.8350 ⎤
Jul : 99.8350 ⎦ 1 %.   0.165 3m Libor.

Printed by Amazon Italia Logistica S.r.l.
Torrazza Piemonte (TO), Italy